AMERICA'S C[illegible] OF AGE

VAN WYCK BROOKS was born in Plainfield, New Jersey, in 1886 and graduated from Harvard in 1907. During the next twenty years he held various journalistic and editorial positions, taught at Stanford University, and was an editor of *The Freeman* and *The American Caravan*. His numerous writings on American literary and cultural life have contributed to make him one of the most influential critics of the past three decades. Winner of the Dial Prize in 1923 and the National Institute of Arts and Letters Gold Medal in 1946, Brooks is generally considered the leader of that school of criticism exemplified by such adherents as H. L. Mencken, Harold Stearns, and Randolph Bourne—a school that has since adopted a much more conservative point of view. Brooks's five-volume history of American literature, *Makers and Finders*, includes *The Flowering of New England*, *New England Indian Summer*, *The World of Washington Irving*, *The Times of Melville and Whitman*, and *The Confident Years*. Among his other well-known works are *The Ordeal of Mark Twain*, *The Pilgrimage of Henry James*, and more recently his two autobiographical works, *Scenes and Portraits* (1954) and *Day of the Phoenix: The Nineteen Twenties I Remember* (1957), and *The Writer in America* (1953) and *John Sloan: A Painter's Life* (1955).

AMERICA'S COMING-OF-AGE

by

Van Wyck Brooks

DOUBLEDAY ANCHOR BOOKS
DOUBLEDAY & COMPANY, INC.
GARDEN CITY, NEW YORK
1958

COVER BY GEORGE GIUSTI

TYPOGRAPHY BY EDWARD GOREY

CONTENTS

PREFACE TO THE REVISED EDITION

OUR dates are brief in these days and therefore we naturally question what authors foist upon us that is old. The essays reprinted here, in a single volume, still have their readers, though few enough; and certain of the ideas that they express still seem to have sufficient life and truth to make them worthy of a new appearance. But a word of explanation is in order. Several of the essays have been reprinted in various collections and anthologies that bring them forward as if they were expressions of the writer's mature mind. Against this a critic has the right to protest. However he may share, in later life, the notions he held in his twenties and early thirties, he is entitled to claim a certain immunity, as regards his numerous errors, in the mere fact that he has ceased to be young. Amiel, defining the critic, the "true critic" that none of us can ever hope to become, remarks, "What years of labour, what study and comparison, are needed to bring the critical judgment to maturity!" Only at fifty, he adds, can the critic "have made the rounds of all the modes of being, only by then can he have mastered all the possible shades of appreciation." Only, one might rather say, when he has lived as long as the Wandering

Jew. As for the early fruit of a critic's mind, it can hardly be other than green. The danger of growing older is that, in losing our greenness, we are also apt to lose the famous *lumen siccum* that parches and offends, as Bacon says, "most men's watery or soft natures," a light that is valuable not because it is dry, but because, being dry, it is closest to fire.

Many, perhaps most, of these ideas I should still be ready to defend, much as I must ask the reader's indulgence for passages that strike an outmoded note, as well as for an oft-recurring mistake, that of attributing to one's own country the faults of human nature in general—perhaps also for an occasional passage that is not as clear as it should be. A style that is not entirely lucid seems to me an insult to one's readers. There is plainly much amiss with the characterizations, owing in part to my sympathy with the time-spirit of the years in which I wrote. In those years we were all engaged in a game that might have been called bearding the prophets, all too ready to say, "Go up, thou baldhead," in the presence of the Elishas of the moment. We had had too much of the old New England poets. We were tired of hearing Longfellow called "the Just" and we inscribed our shards against him, even to the number of six thousand, as the inconstant Athenians used to do. It will be evident that, in Longfellow's case, and that of most of the others—Lowell excepted, and in regard to Lowell my feeling has not greatly changed—I attempted no rounded estimates. I meant merely to brush them lightly, with reference to a point of view that seems to me now sufficiently incomplete. But the tone of my remarks was sometimes rash, even to the point of impudence, a tone caught from my much reading of Heine, who, almost alone, has possessed the secret of being impudent for eternity.

This youthful levity, viewed in later years, has caused me many a blush, as if, in fact, it had not been levity, but an unlovely trait of middle life which Plato calls "the hard little eye of detraction." And so with the attack on Puritanism, which became a bore, and something worse, the more it fell into fumbling hands that could not make the right discriminations. One feels about Puritanism somewhat as Heine felt about the faith. He found his account in attacking it until the party of the attack began to reek of cheese and brandy. At that point, the old cause began to seem very inviting again, and Heine, who had quoted Homer, took to quoting the Bible, like Uncle Tom. As for the Puritan faith, which was never mine, it has ceased to menace any sentient being; and, properly apprehended, it stands for a certain intensity that every writer values.

If, then, I have had a vague horror of having appeared to disparage these older worthies, it is because one finds in them today—in some of them, at least—the large mental bones and the hardy sinews that indicate an important race. One learns with time how difficult it is to maintain the emotional pitch, the zest for intellectual adventure, the balance, the integrity that always mark the classic. Not that I believe in "golden ages"; and may heaven smite the praiser of times past who tries to shame the present with examples of what was never, surely, his own past. The so-called golden ages are merely times when men know how to use their powers and make more of their lives than at other times. There is just as much talent, and just as large a measure of honest striving, in our age as in any other: one would have to live in a tub not to perceive it. Indeed, the irrelevance of these essays is more marked in regard to the present than to the past. They are almost all pre-war essays, and at least three "younger generations"—for with us a lustrum is a generation—have overlapped the one that I describe. To the changes that have marked these later years one can scarcely allude in a preface, even briefly—plainly as they suggest the need of revision whenever one speaks of "America" in relation to "Europe." As for the younger writers, no sentient critic would wish to charge upon them the faults of a previous epoch. If ours is a "homeless generation," as Malcolm Cowley said once—a phrase that does not express self-confidence—it is a very interesting generation, and one that compels a man to use his mind. A homeless generation has obvious needs, however. It needs to be repatriated. It needs to find a home. But where? In what? These are questions that our criticism must soon answer.

America's Coming-of-Age

1915

I. "HIGHBROW" AND "LOWBROW"

> "The middle of humanity thou never knewest,
> but the extremity of both ends."
>
> *Timon of Athens*

I

AT THE time when he was trying to release humanity from the cross of gold on which, as he said, it was crucified, the apostle of Free Silver—representing a point of view that might have been called American—announced that the opinion of all the professors in the United States would not affect his opinions in the least. There was a dilemma!—if one chose to see it. For on the one hand stood a body of supposed experts in economic theory, on the other a man whose profession it was to change and reform economic practice—the one knowing, the other doing; and not only were they at swords' points but an openly avowed and cynical contempt of theory in relation to practical matters was a principal element in the popularity of a popular hero. But was Bryan himself to blame for this? To know anything of the economic theory which is taught in American universities—in many cases compulsorily taught—is to confess that blame is not the right word. For this economic theory is at the least equally cynical. It revolves round and round in its tree-top dream of the economic man; and no matter how much the wind blows, political economy never comes down. Incompatibility, mutual contempt between theory and practice, is in the very nature of the case.

One might extend the illustration to literature, merely substituting one professor for another and putting any typical best-selling novelist in the place of Bryan. It is a peculiar twist in the academic mind to suppose that a writer belongs to literature only when he is dead; living he is, vaguely, something else; and a habitual remoteness from the creative mood has made American professors quite peculiarly academic. "Literature," as distinguished from excellent writing, is, in the American universities, a thing felt to have been done; and, while for all one knows it may continue to be done, the quality in it which makes it literature only comes out, like the quality in wines, with age.

Now I suppose that most of the American novelists in our day are university men; they have learned to regard literature as an august compound of Browning, Ben Jonson and Hesiod; and consequently, when they begin to write, it is in a spirit of real humility that they set themselves to the composition of richly rewarded trash. I am sure of this: it is modesty that lies behind the "best-seller"; and there is an aspect in which the spectacle of writers regarding themselves as humble tradesfolk has a certain charm. But the conception of literature as something, so to speak, high and dry gives to the craft of authorship in America a latitude like that of morality in Catholic countries: so long as the heavenly virtues are upheld mundane virtues may shift as they will. In a word, writers are relieved of responsibility, and, while their ethical conscience remains quite sound, they absolve themselves from any artistic conscience whatsoever. And the worst of it is that precisely these writers of irredeemable trash are often the bright, vigorous, intuitive souls who *could* make literature out of American life. Has it ever been considered how great a knowledge of men, what psychological gifts of the first order their incomparable achievement of popularity implies?

These two attitudes of mind have been phrased once for all in our vernacular as "Highbrow" and "Lowbrow." I have proposed these terms to a Russian, an Englishman and a German, asking each in turn whether in his country there was anything to correspond with the conceptions implied in them. In each case they have been returned to me as quite American, authentically our own, and, I should add, highly suggestive.

What side of American life is not touched by this antithesis? What explanation of American life is more central or more illuminating? In everything one finds this frank acceptance of twin values which are not expected to have anything in common: on the one hand, a quite unclouded, quite unhypocritical assumption of transcendent theory ("high ideals"), on the other a simultaneous acceptance of catchpenny realities. Between university ethics and business ethics, between American culture and American humour, between Good Government and Tammany, between academic pedantry and pavement slang, there is no community, no genial middle ground.

The very accent of the words "Highbrow" and "Lowbrow" implies an instinctive perception that this is a very unsatisfactory state of affairs. For both are used in a derogatory sense. The "Highbrow" is the superior person whose virtue is admitted but felt to be an inept unpalatable virtue; while the "Lowbrow" is a good fellow one readily takes to, but with a certain scorn for him and all his works. And what is true of them as personal types is true of what they stand for. They are equally undesirable, and they are incompatible; but they divide American life between them.

II

They always have divided American life between them; and to understand them one has to go back to the beginning of things—for without doubt the Puritan theocracy is the all-influential fact in the history of the American mind. It was the Puritan conception of the Deity as not alone all-determining but precisely responsible for the practical affairs of the race, as constituting, in fact, the State itself, which precluded in advance any central bond, any responsibility, any common feeling in American affairs and which justified the unlimited centrifugal expediency that has always marked American life. And the same instinct that made against centrality in government made against centrality in thought, against common standards of any kind. The eternal issues the Puritans felt so keenly, the practical issues they experienced so monotonously threw almost no light on one another; there was no middle ground between to mitigate, combine or harmonize them.

So it is that from the beginning we find two main currents in the American mind running side by side but rarely mingling—a current of overtones and a current of undertones—and both equally unsocial: on the one hand, the transcendental current, originating in the piety of the Puritans, becoming a philosophy in Jonathan Edwards, passing through Emerson, producing the fastidious refinement and aloofness of the chief American writers, and resulting in the final unreality of most contemporary American culture; and on the other hand the current of catchpenny opportunism, originating in the practical shifts of Puritan life, becoming a philosophy in Franklin, passing through the American humorists, and resulting in the atmosphere of our contemporary business life.

Thus the literature of the seventeenth century in America is composed in equal parts, one may fairly say, of piety and advertisement; and the revered chronicles of New England had the double effect of proving how many pilgrim souls had been elected to salvation and of populating with hopeful immigrants a land where heaven had proved so indulgent.

For three generations the prevailing American character was compact in one type, the man of action who was also the man of God. Not until the eighteenth century did the rift appear and with it the essential distinction between "Highbrow" and "Lowbrow." It appeared in the two philosophers, Jonathan Edwards and Benjamin Franklin, who shared the eighteenth century between them. In their singular purity of type and in the apparent incompatibility of their aims they determined the American character as a racial fact, and after them the Revolution became inevitable. Channing, Lincoln, Emerson, Whitman, Grant, Webster, Garrison, Edison, Rockefeller, Mrs. Eddy, Woodrow Wilson are all, in one way or another, permutations and combinations of these two grand progenitors of the American mind.

Strange that at the very outset two men should have arisen so aptly side by side and fixed the poles of our national life! For no one has ever more fully than Jonathan Edwards displayed the infinite inflexibility of the upper levels of the American mind, nor has anyone displayed more fully than Franklin the infinite flexibility of its lower levels.

The intellect of Jonathan Edwards was like the Matterhorn, steep, icy and pinnacled. At its base were green slopes and singing valleys filled with little tender wild-flowers—for he was the most lovable of men; but as soon as the ground began to rise in good earnest all this verdurous life came to an abrupt end: not one green or living thing could subsist in that frozen soil, on those pale heights. It was the solitude of logic that led him to see in destiny only a wrathful tyrant and a viper's trail in the mischievous ways of little boys and girls.

I confess to an old-time and so to speak aboriginal affection for this man, so gently solicitous to make up in his daily walk and conversation for the ferocious impulsions of that brain of his. He was even the most romantic of men, as I thought once, and I well remember that immense old musty book of his theology, covered with mildew, with its desert of tiny print, which I carried out with me into the fields and read, in the intervals of bird's-nesting, under the hedgerows and along the borders of the wood: the sun fell for the first time on those clammy old pages and the pallid thoughts that lay in them, and the field-sparrows all about were twittering in a language which, to tell the truth, was no more unintelligible to me. But everything that springs from solitude shines by a light of its own, and Manfred among the Alps was not more lonely than this rapt scholar in his parsonage among the Indians.

There are, however, solitudes and solitudes. Great poets and fruitful thinkers live apart themselves, perhaps, but they have society and the ways of men in their blood. They recollect in tranquility, as it were, gestate, live again, and reveal the last significance of active generations rich in human stuff, in experience, in emotion, in common reason. Nothing like this existed in the background of Jonathan Edwards, no profound and complex race-life. Intellect in him, isolated and not responsible to the other faculties, went on its way unchecked; and he was able to spin his inept sublimities by subtracting from his mind every trace of experience, every touch of human nature as it really was among his innocent countryfolk.

Notoriously, of course, our great Dr. Franklin simplified existence in precisely the opposite way; for the opposite of unmitigated theory is unmitigated practicality. Who can deny that in *Poor Richard* the "Lowbrow" point of view for the first time took definite shape, stayed itself with axioms, and found a sanction in the idea of "policy"? It emerges there full-fledged, in its classical form, a two-dimensional wisdom, a wisdom shorn of overtones, the most accommodating wisdom in the world.

Were ever two views of life more incompatible than these? What indeed could Poor Richard have in common with an Angry God? And what could Bryan have in common with political economy?

III

"Our people," said Emerson, "have their intellectual culture from one country and their duties from another." In how many spheres that phrase can be applied! Desiccated culture at one end and stark utility at the other have created a deadlock in the American mind, and all our life drifts chaotically between the two extremes. Consider, for example, our use of the English language. Literary English in England is naturally a living speech, which occupies the middle of the field and expresses the flesh and blood of an evolving race. Literary English with us is a tradition, just as Anglo-Saxon law with us is a tradition. They persist not as the normal expressions of a race, the essential fibre of which is permanently Anglo-Saxon, but through prestige and precedent and the will and habit of a dominating class largely out of touch with a national fabric unconsciously taking form "out of school." No wonder that our literary style is "pure," that our literary tradition, our tradition especially in oratory and political prose, retains the spirit of the eighteenth century. But at what a cost! At the cost of expressing a popular life that bubbles with energy and spreads and grows and slips away ever more and more from the control of tested ideas, a popular life "with the lid off," which demands an intellectual outlet and finds one in slang, journalism and unmannerly fiction.

After seventy years Carlyle's well-known appeal to Emerson still applies to the spirit of American culture: "For the rest, I have to object still (what you will call objecting against the Law of Nature) that we find you a speaker indeed, but as it were a *Soliloquizer* on the eternal mountain-tops only, in vast solitudes where men and their affairs lie all hushed in a very dim remoteness; and only *the man* and the stars and the earth are visible—whom, so fine a fellow seems he, we could perpetually punch into, and say, 'Why won't you come and help us then? We have terrible need of one man like you down among us! It is cold and vacant up there; nothing paintable but rainbows and emotions; come down and you shall do life-pictures, passions, facts. . . .'"

And what a comment on the same utterance that at this very moment an amiable New Englander should have been painting in Parson Wilbur and Hosea Biglow, respectively, unconscious of any tragic symbolism of things to come, the unbridgeable chasm between literate and illiterate America! Morally, no doubt, in Jaalam, they understood one another and got along very well, as Yankees will. But in Chicago?

IV

To pass now from the social to the personal question, since the question is at bottom a personal one, let us figure to ourselves how this divergence comes about and how it is that our educational system, instead of creating what President Eliot called a "serviceable fellowship" between theory and practice, tends to set them apart and to confirm us all either in the one extreme or in the other.

Let us figure to ourselves a typical American who has grown up, as an American typically does grow up, in a sort of orgy of lofty examples, moralized poems, national anthems and baccalaureate sermons, until he is charged with all manner of ideal purities, ideal honorabilities, ideal femininities, flag-wavings and skyscrapings of every sort—until he comes to feel in himself the hovering presence of all manner of fine potentialities, remote, vaporous and evanescent as a rainbow. All this time, it may fairly be said, he has not been taught to associate himself personally with ends even much lower than these. He has not been taught that life is a legitimate progress toward spiritual or intellectual ends at all. His instincts of acquisition, pleasure, enterprise and desire have in no way been linked and connected with disinterested ends; he has had it embedded in his mind that the getting of a living is not a necessity incidental to some higher and more disinterested end, but that it is the prime and central end. And, as a corollary of this, he has been encouraged to assume that the world is a stamping-ground for his every untrained, greedy and aggressive impulse, that, in short, society is fair prey for what he can get out of it.

Let us imagine that, having grown up in this way, he is sent to college. And here, in order to keep the case a typical one, we shall have to exercise a little discrimination in the choice of a university.

It will not be Harvard, because the ideal of Harvard, as I shall point out, is not a typically modern American ideal. Nor will it be one of the modern utilitarian universities, which have no ideal at all. It will be any one of the others; and when I say this I mean that each of the others is in one way or another a development of the old country college; its ideal, its experience, its tradition spring out of and lead one back to that. Now, among these old colleges Harvard might have been figured as an ever-developing, ever-liberalizing catholicism, of which they were all sectarian offshoots, established on a principle of progressive theological fragmentation, each one defending an orthodoxy its predecessors had outworn or violently setting up in defence of some private orthodoxy of its own. They founded themselves each on a remote dogma or system of dogmas, as their central and sufficient basis, and all their wheels turned in relation to the central theological dynamo. In a sense, this was true also of Harvard, but with a marked difference. For the theologians who founded Harvard were men of action as well. In the seventeenth century, a New England minister was also a politician, and the education of ministers for which Harvard was mainly established implied an education for public affairs as well, and education for society. Thus at the outset the founders of Harvard drove in the wedge of secularism: Harvard had, from the beginning, a sort of national basis, at least among New Englanders, and its dogmatic structure consequently reflected, and shifted with, and accommodated itself to, the currents of national thought. Remaining in touch with society, it educated to a certain extent, relatively to an extraordinary extent, the social function of its students; and it is thus no accident that for many years so large a proportion of the political, the literary and the scientific life of America sprang from it. But in the eighteenth century the conditions under which Harvard was established had ceased to prevail. The minister was no longer a man of affairs—he was a stark theologian, and often of a type which the majority of his flock had outgrown. Yale, Princeton and virtually all the other typically American colleges were founded by men of this type. Jonathan Edwards may figure for them all, the motive which led him to become the president of Princeton being precisely that his New England flock could no longer see the anger of God eye to eye with him. Already in his time the fathers and mothers of young America had submitted to the charms of *Poor Richard's Almanac*; but they seem to have believed that an Angry God might still be a good influence over young America himself.

To return now to our typical case, let us imagine that he makes a typical choice and goes to a typical university. Having arrived there, will he be confronted with an Angry God, or any sort of direct theological dogma? By no means. But there will have remained in the air a certain fragrance and vibration, as if an ideal had passed that way and not stayed, there will be intangible whispers and seductions, there will be a certain faint, rarefied, remote, but curiously pervasive and insistent influence—like the sound of an Æolian harp or the recollection of Plato in some uncouth slum; there will be memories and portraits of many an old metaphysician, white, unearthly, fragile. It will all seem very much as if, the significance of these remote dogmas having evaporated, only the remoteness, in a way, had remained.

One would have to be very insensitive not to feel the quite unbalancing charm of this quality—so different from its comparatively robust Oxford parallel—in the old New England colleges, as in Princeton, Yale and the other universities which have developed out of them; but one cannot help feeling also, I think, something vaguely Circean in it. And in fact, given the preliminary method of bringing-up which I have sketched, what will be its effect in the case we are considering? Suddenly confronted during four years with just this remote influence of ideals, out of which the intellectual structure has evaporated and which never possessed a social structure, will he not find them too vague, too intangible, too unprepared-for to be incorporated into his nature? Certainly ideals of this kind, in this way presented, in this way prepared for, cannot enrich life, because they are wanting in all the elements of personal contact. Wholly dream-like and vaporous, they end by breeding nothing but cynicism and chagrin; and, in becoming permanently catalogued in the mind as impracticable, they lead to a feeling that all ideas are unreal.

Indeed, there is nothing so tragic and so ominous as the familiar saying that college is the happiest time of one's life. Yet perhaps a majority of college men think of their college life in this way. They deliberately put their Golden Age behind them—and, as things are, they know it is behind them. But consider what a comment this is on the American university itself—a place, one would almost say, where ideals are cherished precisely because they are ineffectual, because they are ineptly and mournfully beautiful, because they make one cynical, because they make life progressively uninteresting, because, in effect, they are illusions and frauds and charming lies. There, surely, is the last and the most impenetrable stronghold of Puritanism, refined to the last degree of intangibility, which persists in making the world a world inevitably sordid, basely practical, as if its definition of the ideal were that which has no connection with the world!

Thus far with our typical university man. He has been consistently educated in twin values that are incompatible. The theoretical atmosphere in which he has lived is one that bears no relation to society, the practical atmosphere in which he has lived bears no relation to ideals. Theory has become for him permanently a world in itself, an end in itself; practice has become simply a world of dollars.

Now supposing he is interested in economics, three paths are open to him: either he can give himself once for all to economics, or he can go the way of all flesh, i.e., into business, or he can hesitate between the two, becoming an economist for the time being and eventually going into business.

It is just here, at the moment of choice, that the want of ballast in his education becomes manifest. There is nothing for him but to lurch violently to the one extreme or to the other; and this he does, according as intellect or the sense of action preponderates in his nature. If he is preponderantly intellectual he adopts the first course; that is to say, he dedicates himself to the service of a type of economic theory that bears no relation to this wicked world at all, leaving all the good people who are managing the economic practice of society (and, for the want of him, chiefly muddling it)—leaving all these good people to talk nonsense in the wilderness. If he is preponderantly a man of action, he adopts the second course; that is to say, he dedicates himself to the service of a private end which knows nothing of theory, which is most cynically contemptuous of ideals, flatulent or other, and which is precisely as indifferent to the economic life of society as the professor of economics himself.

Well, good riddance to both of them, one might be inclined to say, except that on second thought the professor and the business man between them hold in their hands so great a part of human destiny. It is the third case that is really interesting and really tragic. For just so far as our typical student is a normal man, just so far as he shares the twin elements of intellect and activity in equal parts, just so far will he be on the fence. The probability is that in this case he will become a professor for as long as he can stand it and then burst into business and become a first-rate millionaire as quickly as possible. The sense of action in him will rebel against the sense of theory, and, finding in theory no basis for action, no relation to action, will press him into a fresh life where the theoretical side of his nature will at least be of some slight use in furthering his own aggrandizement, and that alone.

V

Naturally the question of economics is only typical. Any branch of human activity that is represented by professors—and which is not?—would serve equally well. Human nature itself in America exists on two irreconcilable planes, the plane of stark intellectuality and the plane of stark business; and in the back of its mind lies heaven knows what world of poetry, hidden away, too inaccessible, too intangible, too unreal in fact ever to be brought into the open, or to serve, as the poetry of life should serve, in harnessing thought and action together, turning life into a disinterested adventure.

Whichever way one argues, from the individual to society or from society to the individual, the result is the same. Just as the American attitude towards the State has been the attitude of an oratorical and vague patriotism which has not based itself on a concrete interest in public affairs; just as, in consequence of this, the "invisible government" of business has swept in and taken possession of the field and become the actual government under which we live, overgrowing and supplanting the government we recognize: so also in the case of the individual. The cherishing of ideals that are simply unmapped regions to which nobody has the least intention of building roads, the baccalaureate sermons that are no just, organic comment on the educational system that precedes them—precisely these themselves strengthen the forces from below; the invisible government of self-interest, built up carefully from the beginning by maxim and example, fills the vacuum a disinterested purpose ought to have occupied.

Thirty or forty years ago, it would have been generally assumed that the only hope for American society lay in somehow lifting the "Lowbrow" elements to the level of the "Highbrow" elements. But the realism of contemporary thought makes it plain that the mere idealism of university ethics, the loftiness of what is called culture, the purity of so-called Good Government, left to themselves, produce a glassy inflexible priggishness on the upper levels that paralyzes life. It is equally plain that the lower levels have a certain humanity, flexibility, tangibility which are indispensable in any programme: that Tammany has quite as much to teach Good Government as Good Government has to teach Tammany, that slang has quite as much in store for culture as culture has for slang—that the universities, while emphatically not becoming more "practical," must base their disinterestedness on human, moral, social, artistic and personal needs, impulses and experience.

But society cannot become humane of itself; and it is for this reason that the movements of reform are so external and so superficial. The will-to-reform springs from a conviction *ex post facto*. It suggests the frame of mind of business men who retire at sixty and collect pictures. Nothing so exemplifies it as the spectacle of Andrew Carnegie spending three-quarters of his life in providing steel for battleships and the last quarter of it in trying to abolish war. He himself surely was not conscious of any inward revolution; plainly with him as with others the will to create disorder, or what amounts to this, and the will to reform it sprang from the same inner condition of mind. The impetus of reform is evidently derived from the hope that a sufficient number of reformers can be trained and brought into the field to match the forces of business—the one group cancelling the other group. The ideal of reform, in short, is the attainment of zero.

Nothing is more absurd than to attack business as such. But the motives and circumstances of business vary from age to age, and there is a world of difference between industry conceived as a social process and trade conceived as a private end. A familiar distinction between the nineteenth and the twentieth centuries is that the problem of civilization is no longer the problem of want but the problem of surplus. Roughly speaking, the hereditary American class—the prevailing class, I mean—is faced with the problem not of making money but of spending it; the prevailing American class is in a position of relative, but relatively great, economic freedom, and under these conditions it is plain that in them economic self-assertion ("enterprise") has become to a large extent a vicious anachronism. But force of habit, the sheer impetus and ground-swell of an antiquated pioneering spirit, finds them with no means of personal outlet except, on the one hand, a continued economic self-assertion and on the other a reckless overflow of surplus wealth that takes the form of doing what everybody else does, and doing it as much more so as possible.

Because it was for so long the law of the tribe, economic self-assertion still remains to most Americans a sort of moral obligation, while self-fulfillment still looks like a pretty word for selfishness. Yet self-fulfillment through science, or literature, or mechanics, or industry itself—the working out of one's own personality, one's own inventiveness through forms of activity that are directly social, as all these activities are directly social, gives a man, through his very sociality, through the feeling he has that, as a good workman, he is coöperating with all other good workmen, a life-interest apart from his rewards. And as this principle is diffused and understood, the incentive is withdrawn from economic self-assertion, a relative competence being notoriously satisfying to the man whose prime end is the fulfilling of his own creative instincts; and the wealth of the world is already socialized.

One cannot have personality, one cannot have the expressions of personality so long as the end of society is an impersonal end like the accumulation of money. For the individual whose personal end varies too greatly from the end of the mass of men about him suffers acutely and becomes abnormal; indeed, he actually cannot accomplish anything healthily fine at all. The best and most disinterested individual can only express the better intuitions and desires of his age and place; there must be some sympathetic touch between him and some visible or invisible host about him, since the mind is a flower that has an organic connection with the soil from which it springs.

The only serious approach to society is the personal approach, and the quickening realism of contemporary social thought is at bottom simply a restatement for the mass of commercialized men, and in relation to issues that directly concern men as a whole, of those personal instincts that have been the essence of art, religion, literature—the essence of personality itself—since the beginning of things. It will remain of the least importance to patch up politics, to become infected with social consciousness, or to do any of the other easy popular contemporary things unless, in some way, personality can be made to release itself on a middle plane between vaporous idealism and self-interested practicality; unless, in short, self-fulfillment as an ideal can be substituted for self-assertion as an ideal. On the economic plane, this implies socialism;

on every other plane it implies something which a majority of Americans in our day certainly do not possess—an object in living.

VI

It is perhaps just as well that Cervantes lived and died in Spain three hundred years ago. Had he been born an American of the twentieth century he might have found the task of satire an all too overwhelming one. Yet his fable, which has its personal bearing in all men always, has in America a social bearing that is perhaps unique. Don Quixote is the eternal "Highbrow" under a polite name, just as Sancho Panza is the eternal "Lowbrow"; and if the adorable Dulcinea is not a vision of the night and a daily goal in the mind of our professors, then there is no money in Wall Street. One admits the charm of both extremes, the one so fantastically above, the other so fantastically below the level of right reason; to have any kind of relish for muddled humanity is necessarily to feel the charm of both extremes. But where is all that is real, where is personality and all its works, if it is not essentially somewhere, somehow, in some not very vague way, between?

II. "OUR POETS"

I

It is a principle that shines impartially on the just and on the unjust that once you have a point of view all history will back you up. Everything, no doubt, depends upon evidence; and considering the case which has been outlined in the last chapter, an appeal to American literature, if literature really does record the spirit of a people, is an appeal that leads, I think, to evidence of a material sort.

Something, in American literature, has always been wanting—every one, I think, feels that. Aside from the question of talent, there is not, excepting Walt Whitman, one American writer who comes home to a modern American with that deep, moving, shaking impact of personality for which one turns to the abiding poets and writers of the world. A certain density, weight and richness, a certain poignancy, a "something far more deeply interfused," simply is not there.

Above all, the Americanism of our old writers appears to have had no faculty of development and adaptation. With the death of Emerson, Lowell, Holmes and their group, something in the American mind really came to an end. The generation that has passed since then is a generation which has produced no indisputable leader of thought and letters, which has destroyed the coherence of the old American circle of ideas, and left us at the height of the second immigration among the chaotic raw materials of a perhaps altogether new attitude of mind.

It is, in fact, the plain, fresh, homely, impertinent, essentially innocent old America that has passed, and in its passing the allegory of Rip Van Winkle has been filled with a new meaning. Hendrik Hudson and his men, we see, have begun another game of bowls, and the reverberations are heard in many a summer thunderstorm; but they have been miraculously changed into Jews, Lithuanians, Magyars, and German socialists. Rip is that old innocent America which has fallen asleep and which hears and sees in a dream the movement of peoples, the thunder of alien wants. And when after twenty years he awakens again, stretches his cold rheumatic limbs, and discovers the long white beard, he will once more set out for home. But when he arrives will he be recognized?

What emotions pass through an hereditary American when he calls to mind the worthies who figured in that ubiquitous group of "Our Poets" which occupied once so prominent a place in so many domestic interiors! Our Poets were commonly six in number, kindly, grey-bearded, or otherwise grizzled old men. One recalls a prevailing six, with variations. Sometimes a venerable historian was included, a novelist or so, and even Bayard Taylor.

Nothing could make one feel so like a prodigal son as to look at that picture. So much for the first glance, the first quick impression after one has come home to it from the far wanderings of an ordinary profane existence. But more complicated emotions supervene. What a world within a world that picture summons up! Frankly, we feel in ourselves, we are no longer so fortunate as in those days. It could really have been said of us then, as it cannot now be said at all, that as a folk we had won a certain coherence, a certain sort of ripeness in the better part of ourselves, which was reflected in the coherence of our men of letters. Whittier, for example, was a common basis, and a very sweet and elevating basis, for a national programme of emotions the like of which no poet since his time has been able to compass. One recalls that fact, so full of meaning; and then, deep down, a forgotten world sweeps back over one, a world of memory, sentiment and association, a world of influences the most benign—like a mournful autumn wind stirring in forsaken places. But sooner or later the ordinary profane existence reasserts itself; and we have to put it to ourselves with equal frankness—has any one of these men, or any one of these influences, the power at bottom to make it less profane? The most benign sentiment in the world will not do so unless it has in it that which grips in some way at the root of personality.

It is no use to go off into a corner with American literature, as most of the historians have done, in a sulky, private sort of way, taking it for granted that if we give up world values we are entitled to our own little domestic rights and wrongs, criticism being out of place by the fireside. "But oh, wherever else I am accounted dull," wrote Cowper in one of his letters, "let me pass for a genius at Olney." This is the method of the old-fashioned camp in American criticism, just as the method of the contemporary camp is the method of depreciative comparison with supposedly better folk than our own.

The only fruitful approach is the personal approach, and to me, at least, Thoreau, Emerson, Poe and Hawthorne are possessions forever. This does not alter the fact that if my soul were set on the accumulation of dollars not one of them would have the power to move me from it. And this I take to be a suggestive fact. Not one of them, not all of them, have had the power to move the soul of America from the accumulation of dollars; and when one has said this one has arrived at some sort of basis for literary criticism.

Plainly enough, during what has been called the classical period of American literature, the soul of America did not wish to be moved from the accumulation of dollars; plainly enough, the pioneering instinct of economic self-assertion was the law of the tribe. And if the New England writers were homogeneous with the American people as no other group, scarcely any other individual, has been since, it is equally plain that they themselves and all their works must have accorded with the law of the tribe. The immense, vague cloud-canopy of idealism which hung over the American people during the nineteenth century was never permitted, in fact, to interfere with the practical conduct of life.

Never permitted, I say, although it is a more accurate explanation that, being essentially impersonal itself, the essence of this idealism lay in the very fact that it had and could have no connection with the practical conduct of life. The most successful and famous writers, Bryant and Longfellow, for example, promoted this idealism, being, so far as one can see, generally satisfied with the ordinary practices of society: they tacitly accepted the peculiar dualism that lies at the root of our national point of view. Emerson's really equivocal individualism on the one hand asserted the freedom and self-reliance of the spirit and on the other appeared to justify the unlimited private expediency of the business man. And as a suggestive corollary of this, the two principal artists in American literature, Poe and Hawthorne, were out of touch with society as few other artists in the world had been before: to their contemporaries they seemed spectral and aloof, scarcely human, and equally marked was the reaction upon their work of a world to them essentially unreal.

Granting these facts, and granting the still more significant fact of the absence from our literature of that deep, moving, shaking impact of personality which would have brought it into more permanent touch with American life, I do not see how we can escape the general axiom: that a society whose end is impersonal and anti-social cannot produce an ideal reflex in literature which is personal and social, and conversely, that the ideal reflex in literature produced by such a society will be unable to educate its own personal and social instincts. In effect, an examination of American literature will show, I think, that those of our writers who have possessed a vivid personal genius have been paralyzed by the want of a social background, while those who have possessed a vivid social genius have been equally unable to develop their personalities.

II

And here at the outset a distinction must be drawn between what may be called the literature of necessity and absolute literature. It is perfectly plain that in one aspect literature is a simple cog in the machinery of life. The first generation of American writers were like prudent women who, having moved into a new house, energetically set to work laying down carpets, papering the walls, cutting and hanging the most appropriate window-curtains, and pruning the garden—making it, in short, a place of reasonable charm and contentment.

Than Washington Irving, for example, no one was ever more satisfied with things as they are; prosperity in others aroused in him the most benignant emotions, and there is a description by him of a smiling river farm with its fat hens and waddling pigs which rises to a sort of placid ecstasy. In recollection, one confuses the pigs with little cherubim, and, as for the farm itself, one wonders why (or indeed whether) angels have not settled there.

The effect of this idyllic treatment is precisely that of the first warm blaze in a newly constructed hearth. It takes away the sense of chill; the room becomes at once cozy and cheerful, and we enjoy the prospect of spending an evening in it.

That is at least a principal element in the work of Irving, Cooper, Bryant and Longfellow. When these men ceased writing, the towns, the woods, the wild-flowers, even the bare and meagre history of America were clothed with memories and associations. It was possible to feel them all, and even to muse upon them. The characters of Cooper lighted up a little fringe of the black uncut forest; they linked the wilderness with our own immemorial human world, just as the little figures Piranesi put in his engravings not only give the scale of his Roman ruins and relate them to the observer's eye but also arouse the sense of historical connections, the sense of pathos and of man's destiny.

When these authors wrote of Europe their essential motive was the same as when they wrote of America. Irving's English essays at bottom, as he himself declares, were deliberately intended to place England and America on a basis of mutual good will—a motive, in the proper sense, political. Longfellow never forgot in Europe that he was on leave of absence and that in gathering specimens he was to bear in mind the soil to which they were to be transplanted. There was nothing in heaven or earth he was not able to prune and fertilize into harmony with the New England temperature; and who will deny that he in turn altered that temperature, warmed and gladdened it—that he came back as a kind of gulf-stream to our frost-bitten civilization, which has been more humane ever since?

III

But out of this essential motive of the first generation of American writers a second motive arises. They were moralists, they were shot through and through with all manner of baccalaureate ideals; and this fact opens them to a different sort of treatment. For this let Longfellow and Bryant suffice, for they are typical.

Longfellow is to poetry, in large measure, what the barrel-organ is to music; approached in a hypercritical spirit, he simply runs on, and there is an end to the matter. But nobody dreams of criticizing Longfellow from the point of view of "mere literature": the human head and the human heart alike revolt from that. His personal sanction is rightly a traditional one, and the important thing is to see him as a beautifully typical figure and to see just what he typifies.

To Longfellow the world was a German picture-book, never detaching itself from the softly coloured pages. He was a man of one continuous mood: it was that of a flaxen-haired German student on his *wanderjahr* along the Rhine, under the autumn sun—a sort of expurgated German student—ambling among ruined castles and reddening vines, and summoning up a thousand bright remnants of an always musical past. His was an eminently Teutonic nature of the old school, a pale-blue melting nature; and white hair and grandchildren still found him with all the confused emotion, the charming sadness, the indefinite high proposals of seventeen; perhaps it was because they had never been opposed, never put to the test in that so innocently successful existence of his that they persisted without one touch of disillusion, one moment of chagrin.

But frankly what preparation is a life like this for the poet whose work it is to revivify a people? The most telling thing one knows about Longfellow is that, having remarked that "Carlyle was one of those men who sacrifice their happiness to their work," he himself was well content in later life to surrender the greater part of his time and energies to writing autographs and entertaining children. Here certainly the personal sanction oversteps the mark, just as it does in the case of indulgent politicians who exhibit their gratitude and warm-heartedness by feathering the nests of all their friends and cousins. Longfellow had an unerring eye for the "practical application" that lurks in every shred of romance, totally unable to elude the agile moralist, but the value of his moral promptings is just in proportion to the pressure behind them—and where was the pressure? His morals and ideals were, in fact, simply a part of the pretty picture-book, just as they are at seventeen: if they had not been so they would never have been laid on the shelf.

But the "practical application" cannot be dismissed

in this way; and if the personal sanction is disarming in relation to Longfellow, the case is otherwise with Bryant, a hard-headed man. To Bryant the moral ending was no half absent-minded flourish of the colour-brush—it was a tough Puritan reality; and Bryant's use of the moral ending is emblematic not merely, as in Longfellow's case, of the vacuity and impermanence of so much American idealism, but also of the corollary of these—the failure of Americans in general to develop and express their personality in and through their work.

Bluntly, the use of a moral ending means that the poet is unwilling to leave his effect to the emotion conveyed in the poem itself; he must needs intellectualize this emotion at the close, and show you that it is only used, like cheese in a mouse-trap, to entice the reader into a usually disagreeable fact, for which the whole exists. And this procedure is full of meaning. For not the emotion, not the expression of personality, but the ulterior object is the essential issue in the mind of the poet: not life, but success, or salvation. And the same principle operates here and renders the result equally barren as in work which is done mainly for the ulterior object of making money, in thought which exists merely for the ulterior object of proving something. The excellence and fruitfulness of anything consists in our loving and enjoying it, in our expressing our personality through it. Real poetry springs from the assumption that the spectacle is its own reward, that feeling, happy or unhappy, is final: it is concerned, as Shelley pointed out, not with effects and applications, which are temporary, but with causes, which are permanent. The moral ending is simply a rigid and impersonal intellectualization of life, which is, consequently, out of touch with the motives that really determine men.

For this reason Bryant was scarcely a personality; he was, to be exact, a somewhat eminent personage. After his thirtieth year he was miraculously changed, not into stone, but into wood—he was as bald, as plain, as immovable, so to say, as an old settee. He had no elasticity, no sense of play either in words, ideas or emotions; two or three poetic forms sufficed him; even as a journalist he was abstract. One sees him during sixty years perambulating Broadway with that old blue cotton umbrella of his, the very picture of a spare old Puritan patriarch, with his big muscular joints. And all about him one sees that spry, flimsy New York of the forties and fifties and sixties—the New York of *Nothing to Wear* and N. P. Willis. It is these gulfs of contrast which let one into the secret of American humour.

For this old man with his palsied gift, pursued for two generations by glimpses of the grave, who yet had within him an incomparable vigour and who, past eighty, put Homer into English—this old man was himself Homeric amid that spawn of decadent Byronism which made up the so-called Knickerbocker school. New York has never possessed dignity—one loves the many-headed beast for a thousand other reasons than that; but it has achieved a sort of Napoleonic right to despise dignity, and it has come to possess its secrets. In the thirties and forties it possessed no secrets at all —it was the centre of an ingenuous nation which had only just learned to be worldly, which the lightest zephyr from London or Paris set fluttering, over which every ripple of fashion broke into a spray of tinsel.

IV

So much is necessary to give Poe what he badly needs, a naturalistic setting: Poe himself, who emerges from this New York of his time like a wreck at sea with its black spars etched against a sort of theatrical sunset. Ironical and sinister as he is, he is by no means "out of space, out of time," if by space we mean New York and by time the second quarter of the nineteenth century. The little imitation Byrons who swarmed about him wrote of haunted Gothic castles, Poe wrote *The House of Usher;* Bianca, Giordano, Ermengarde, Elfrida, Asthene, Zophiel were the human properties of their prose and verse, scarcely to be distinguished from the Madeleines and Eleanores, the Eulalies and Annabels, the Israfels and Al Aaraafs of Poe; they also lived in a world of moan and a world of moonlight. Madness, irreparable farewells, dungeons, assignations, premature burials, hidden treasures, exotic musical instruments, prophetic night-birds —these things were of the time and very particularly, since New York provided them with an additional unreality, of the place.

Poe took this bric-à-brac seriously: that is always a distinction and it is Poe's distinction. The tacit conventionalites of the romantic epoch became in him objects of a fierce intellectual concentration. In the comfortable safety of good and abundant food, friendly talk, substantial occupation, his contemporaries amused themselves with spectres, Oriental mysteries, hasheesh and madness: Poe was the delirium that followed. He was a Byron without scope of action and without purging emotions.

Superficially at least he was not conscious of being out of his element. In those critical essays in which he is so accessible and so honest and has so many disagreeable things to say about his contemporaries, it is never the false taste, never the epoch that displeases him. He likes *The Dying Rosebud's Lament* by Mrs. Fanny Osgood; what irritates him is bad grammar, bad rhymes and plagiarism. Nor is there the least indication that he thought America provincial, or bourgeois, or depressing to a man of talent. That indeed is an element in the strength of all the American writers of the old school; an instinct of self-preservation kept them at home in spirit; so much of the missionary element was of the texture of what they had to say that a tinge of the cosmopolitan would have neutralized their best effects, would have rendered them personally, as it has certainly rendered Lowell, a little characterless, a little indistinct. But it is a rather disconcerting fact in relation to the theory that Poe is a kind of supersensual enigma, who might have lived with equal results in Babylon or Sioux City. At his second-best, in prose and verse, he is precisely at one both in tone and execution with his intellectual surroundings. At his best it is this outworn bric-à-brac that is transfigured, just as the suburban bibliolatry of England is transfigured in the drawings of Blake. The important thing is to consider what this bric-à-brac is transfigured into, and why, and what it means.

Since the days of the alchemists no one has produced more than Poe the effects of damnation, no one has been more conscious of being damned. In his pages the breath of life never stirs: crimes occur that do not reverberate in the human conscience, there is laughter that has no sound, there is weeping without tears, there is beauty without love, there is love without children, trees grow that bear no fruit, flowers that have no fragrance—it is a silent world, cold, blasted, moon-struck, sterile, a devil's heath. Only a sensation of intolerable remorse pervades it.

Poe is commonly called unreal; it is justly said of him that he never touches the general heart of man, that perhaps of all writers who have lived he has the least connection with human experience. Nothing is more sinister about Poe, for instance, than his tacit acceptance of common morals; you might even say that he is rigidly conventional, if you did not feel that he is conventional merely because the moral world no more exists for him than it exists for a black stone. If you could prove a vicious motive in him, as from certain points of view you can prove a vicious motive in Baudelaire, you might, even in that, establish some fusion between him and the common reason of humankind. Orchids are as much a part of the vegetable kingdom as potatoes, but Poe is an orchid made out of chemicals. Magic is always so; it has the sinister quality of a force operating outside nature, without any relation to human values.

No European can exist without a thousand subterranean relationships; but Americans can so exist, Americans do so exist. Edison, for example, resembles Poe as a purely inventive mathematical intellect, and with Edison, as with Poe, one feels that some electric fluid takes the place of blood; one feels that the greatest of inventors cannot be called a scientist at all, that his amazing powers over nature are not based on any philosophical grasp of the laws of nature, that he is in temperament a mechanic rather than a philosopher. His faculty is to that of Darwin, for example, what fish is to flesh—to the philosophical animal man, he is more incomprehensible; and for all the beneficence of his faculty he is himself a kind of prodigious salamander. Poe is a mechanic of the same sort. He has discovered in literature the chemical secret of life. He has produced chemical men, chemical emotions, chemical landscapes; in *Eureka* he has produced even a chemical philosophy so much like real philosophy that until you try to feel it you will never guess it the most sterile of illusions. For this reason the highly-coloured effects that light up his tales and his poems are lurid and metallic. The sinister greens and reds and yellows are not, one feels, the flames of honest wood and coal.

To explain all this it is not enough to say that he had a spectral nature, that Emerson and Jonathan Edwards and Hawthorne had spectral natures, that theosophy and Christian Science suggest that this quality is a typical American quality. So much is probably true, but more is required; and to approach Poe is to approach those mysteriously fascinating thaumaturgic elements in nature which are responsible for most of the fraudulent science in the world. One treads warily on the outer edges of psychology, and I suppose it is not accurately known what forces of the mind were involved in mediæval witchcraft, in alchemy, in the conception of Mephistopheles. But certainly to the Middle Ages the intelligence in and for itself was felt to be a maleficent force: Mephistopheles himself in the old legends is nothing other than pure intellect, irresponsible and operating independently of life. Necessarily therefore to him faith, love and hope are illusions, and he is the negation of the soul. Above all, it is the secret of creating life for which in the mediæval imagination souls were bartered to the devil: one obtained the power of competing with God at the price of a perpetual consciousness of one's own damnation. These are dark ways; but one emerges into the region of knowledge when one affirms that, by their mental twist, witches and alchemists were not convicted by society any more than they were convicted in themselves of having done the unpardonable and the irreparable. And certain it is that Poe experienced in his own imagination this power and this damnation. His haunted face, his driven life, the barren world that he has built and peopled, the horror of his accustomed mood, the inextinguishable obscure remorse that broods in him unite in this fact.

The power he still exerts is an hysterical rather than a literary power, and who can say what it signifies? But one thing seems true, with regard alike to witchcraft, alchemy and Poe, that the mind can work healthily only when it is essentially in touch with the society of its own age. No matter into what unknown region it presses, it must have a point of relativity in the common reason of its time and place. Poe, having nothing in common with the world that produced him, constructed a little parallel world of his own, withered at the core, a silent comment. It is this that makes him so sterile and so inhuman; and he is himself, conversely, the most menacing indictment of a society which is not also an all-embracing organism.

V

Poe and Hawthorne, certainly, were much more of a common stock in temperament than the New York and New England of their time. The temperament which in Poe is at once vulgarized by vulgar circumstances and pressed up into the intellect is diffused in the character and work of Hawthorne; the harsher lights are neutralized, the familiar world reappears again—but is it the familiar world? Hawthorne's talent is like a phosphorescent pool; you touch it, you move your hand there and a thousand subdued elusive lights dance through it, but before you can fix your eye upon one of them it has retreated through the clear water, the still depths that are so impenetrable.

No other talent is of so shining a purity as Hawthorne's—scarcely one other so light, so inevitable, so refined, so much a perfectly achieved intention. He models in mist as the Greeks modelled in marble; his beings take shape in the imagination with a sunlit perfection, but only for a moment; they melt and pass; the air is filled with a phantasmagorical movement of shapes, grouping themselves, putting on corporeality as a garment and at the same time dissolving into the nebulous background. It is a cloud pageant and the clouds are of opal dust. The Puritan conscience in Hawthorne is like some useful Roman vessel of glass which has been buried for centuries in the earth and which comes forth at last fragile as a dragon-fly's wing, shot through with all the most exquisite colours. He is the most opalescent of writers, and each of his books is an opal of a different type: crimson, purple and emerald cross and recross *The Marble Faun*, and all the most fleeting tints of pale yellow, pale green and pearly white shimmer through *The Blithedale Romance*, with a single strain of tragic red passing athwart it in the character of Zenobia. A hundred times the world of Hawthorne seems the familiar world, but just as we imagine we have gained a foothold there a wand passes over it, a wall is removed behind it—it has become a world within a world.

This leads one almost to forget that Hawthorne's range is limited, that his gift is meagre and a little anæmic, that his poetry is not quite the same thing as wisdom. For if, like the greatest poets, he sees life as a fable, with a fable's infinitely multiplied correspondences, he feels it rather as a phantom than as a man. This being who passed twelve years of his youth in a solitary, close-curtained room, walking abroad only in the twilight or after the sun had set, was himself a phantom in a phantom world. Observe how he treats any one of his typical characters, the elfish little Priscilla, for example. He is describing the rumours current among her neighbours and how they believed that "the sun, at midday, would shine through her; in the first grey of the twilight, she lost all the distinctness of her outline; and, if you followed the dim thing into a dark corner, behold, she was not there." And he goes on: "There was a lack of human substance in her; it seemed as if, were she to stand up in a sunbeam, it would pass right through her figure, and trace out the cracked and dusty window-panes upon the naked floor." Could anything be more exquisite? Could anything more entirely fail to connect with reality in a practical Yankee world?

It is the natural corollary of this that Hawthorne himself, as a social being (in his opinions especially—for he did not abstain from opinions), was more than commonly conventional. It is natural that this most deeply planted of American writers, who indicates more than any other the subterranean history of the American character, should have recoiled from every attempt to change, rectify or spiritualize society. His talent was a kind of Prospero's isle quite outside the world he lived in. It was *kept* outside that world by his own infallible instinct of artistic self-preservation. The comment he puts into the mouth of Miles Coverdale, apropos of the "philanthropist" Hollingsworth, is really his own comment on the society in which he found himself: "The moral which presents itself to my reflections, as drawn from Hollingsworth's character and errors, is simply this—that admitting what is called philanthropy, when adopted as a profession, to be often useful by its energetic impulse to society at large, it is perilous to the individual whose ruling passion, in one exclusive channel, it thus becomes. It ruins, or is fearfully apt to ruin, the heart, the rich juices of which God never meant should be pressed violently out, and distilled into alcoholic liquor, by an unnatural process, but should render life sweet, bland and gently beneficent, and insensibly influence other hearts and other lives to the same blessed end."

Hawthorne was right with regard to the society of his day, but consider what he lost and what we have lost by it. It is not the business of an artist as such to change society; and if Hawthorne held aloof from everything that stood for movement in his time, that was the price of being sensitively organized in an age of rude, vague, boisterous, dyspeptic, incoherent causes. The fact that Hawthorne and Poe were the only two eminent minds of their age to which Transcendentalism was profoundly repugnant is the surest proof that they alone possessed the full and the right artistic instinct. They had to do what they could in society as it was—and what happened? Outwardly accepting it, but having nothing in common with it, they neither enriched society nor were enriched by it. They were driven to create and inhabit worlds of their own—diaphanous private worlds of mist and twilight.

VI

One finds it impossible to approach the question of Transcendentalism—the thing itself, and Emerson, Margaret Fuller, the Dial, Brook Farm, and all the other permutations and combinations of it—without first of all expelling a persistent spleen, and then submitting oneself to long explanations. So much truth, so much talent, so much of the American character is involved in that queer miasmatical group of lunar phenomena, in which philosophy, self-culture, politics, art, social reform and religion were all mixed up and all felt to be, in some vague way, the same thing. One angel no doubt can stand quite comfortably on the point of a pin, but when a whole battalion of angels attempt to occupy this identical space there is usually war in heaven.

It is plain enough that the Transcendentalists had no sense of the relationship that exists between theory and practice, between the abstract and the concrete. The world they lived in was an excessively concrete world—a world of isolated facts. The white wooden houses, the farms, the patches of wood, the self-contained villages, each with its town-meeting, the politician, the minister, the lawyer, the merchant were, in fact, very much what Emerson called his own sentences, "infinitely repellent particles"; they had, relatively speaking, nothing in common but the Yankee temperament—and the quality of this common temperament was to be as *un*common, as individual and as different, as possible. There was no fusion, no operative background of social forces; there were no unwritten laws. The experience of New England was an experience of two extremes—bare facts and metaphysics: the machinery of self-preservation and the mystery of life. Experience of the world, of society, of art, the genial middle ground of human tradition existed only as an appetite. Painting, sculpture, architecture were represented by engravings; history, travel, world-politics, great affairs in general were represented by books. The habit of looking at things in the abstract, native to the old

Calvinistic temper, was extended over the range of social and intellectual interests, partly as a result of isolation, partly because of the highly tenuous connection between these interests and the primitive actualities of life as New Englanders knew it.

German philosophy, released over the world, inevitably came to port in this society, for above everything else it appeared to let one into the secret of universal experience. If, under the influence of this philosophy, one sat up late enough at night one could be an Alexander, a Plato, a Raphael or (in Boston) a Washington Allston, without moving out of one's chair. It is true, one gained no territory and painted no pictures by this method, but one at least placed oneself at the seat of operations where all these wonderful things occur.

This accounts for the peculiar flavour of that old New England culture, so dry, so crisp, so dogmatic, so irritating. Having entered wholly through the brain in the form of general propositions, without any checking from observation or experience, it seems curiously inverted, curiously unreal. Witness, for example, that strange faraway tone in which Emerson so often and so characteristically refers to "Plato and Paul and Plutarch, Augustine, Spinoza, Chapman, Beaumont and Fletcher," or "the remains of Phidias, the Apollo, the Jove, the paintings and statues of Michael Angelo, the works of Canova." There would be something quite ludicrous in this glimpse of St. Paul, Fletcher, Phidias and Spinoza arm in arm if one felt that Emerson had ever realistically pictured to himself these men as they individually were. To him they were all thrice-purified ghosts, ghosts of the printed page; the associations of the tavern, the synagogue, the drawing-room had fallen from their spirits in the mind of

Emerson as utterly as from their bodies in the grave. To him they were exceptionally fine manifestations of the Over-Soul; philosophy like death had levelled them and had, as entirely, removed them from the region of terrestrial society, literature and art. So also in effect when Margaret Fuller comes to the conclusion that "colour is consecrate to passion and sculpture to thought." Having thus as it were removed the whole question to another planet, she is able to present us further with a jewel of criticism like this: "The Prophets and Sibyls are for the Michael Angelos. The Beautiful is Mr. Allston's dominion." (Statements that make one feel a thousand years old.) Yet this result is inevitable when works of art are approached not through the eye but through the mind: the element of taste, the perceptions of sense, once laid aside, there is no gulf between Phidias and Canova, between Michael Angelo and Washington Allston.

And then consider Emerson's style—that strange fine ventriloquism, that attenuated voice coming from a great distance. If it is irritating, as many readers find it, if it is filled with assertions that fairly insist upon being contradicted, it is because so often Emerson is abstract at the wrong times and concrete at the wrong times, because he has so little natural sense of the relation between the abstract and the concrete. Take, for instance, a typical sentence like this: "Archimedes will look through your Connecticut machine, at a glance, and judge of its fitness"—to which the inevitable reply is, that Archimedes will do nothing of the kind: I no more possess a Connecticut machine than Archimedes will put on mortality again to look through it. Is it unfair to literalize these metaphorical affirmations of Emerson? Of course, one understands that to him "Archimedes" is merely a name for that particular aspect of the Over-Soul which broods over machinery, while my "Connecticut machine" means any human device that will serve to exhibit its powers of divination. But a prose that violates the actual overmuch, a prose in which the poetic effect is more than a heightened version of the actual is, I think, a prose one is entitled to find irritating. Furthermore, Emerson's method of simply announcing as axiomatic what is in his mind is justified only by the possession of a faculty which he does not always possess, the faculty of hitting the nail inevitably on the head. Let one example suffice: "Shelley, though a poetic mind, is never a poet. His muse is uniformly imitative; all his poems composite. A good English scholar he is, with ear, taste, and memory; much more, he is a character full of noble and prophetic traits; but imagination, the original, authentic fire of the bard, he has not." Does this really suggest Shelley?

Emerson's artistic impressions are often of this hit-or-miss character; he can write page after page about a painter or a poet with scarcely one intelligibly apt utterance. Much the same is true of Carlyle and Ruskin, and for the same reason, that alike they all refer art to an extra-artistic standard. But Carlyle and Ruskin are concrete enough in their own wilful ways, while Emerson is persistently abstract. He never lingers in the bodily world, he is always busy to be off again; and if he takes two or three paces on the earth they only serve to warm him for a fresh aërial adventure. Thus the essay on *Illusions* opens with an account of a day spent in the Mammoth Cave in Kentucky, and after the second sentence he continues in this way: "I lost the light of one day. I saw high domes, and bottomless pits; heard the voice of unseen waterfalls," etc. That is not the tone of descriptive writing; a glamour like that of oratory has fallen over it; phrase by phrase the effect is heightened and generalized under the reader's eye; we see how impatient he is to get to the real business and that the experience is already dimmed and evaporated by the approaching application.

The truth is that Emerson was imperfectly interested in human life; he cared little for experience or emotion, possessing so little himself. "He generally addressed me as if I were wholly impersonal," writes one of his disciples, who records an observation of Emerson that he "could never turn a dozen pages of *Don Quixote* or Dickens without a yawn." This accounts for the way in which his thoughts inevitably flew for refuge to capital letters, emerging as Demonology, Creeds, Prudence, the Ideal, abstractions all. His point of view was formed very early; all his later books are sprouts from the first one, and there is little indication of growth, imbibition or excursiveness beyond his original boundaries. If he remained open, he was open only as it were at the top; and before he was thirty-five he seems to have acquired that fixed, benignant, musing smile which implies the consciousness of having solved one's problem and which is usually accompanied by a closure of the five senses.

I say all this without prejudice to Emerson's position in the world of the spirit. There he truly lived and lives, and of all American writers he alone appears to me to have proved the reality of that world and to have given some kind of basis to American idealism.

But Emerson's idealism was double-edged: it was concerned not merely with the spiritual life of the individual, but also with the individual in society, with the "conduct of life." This latter aspect of his teaching was in fact the secret of his contemporary influence.

For if the logical result of a thorough-going, self-reliant individualism in the world of the spirit is to become a saint, it is no less true that the logical result of a thorough-going, self-reliant individualism in the world of the flesh is to become a millionaire. And in fact it would be hard to say whether Emerson more keenly relished saintliness or shrewdness. Both qualities he himself possessed in a high degree, as only an American can; and if on one side of his nature he was a most lonely and beautiful seer, the records of his life prove that he lacked none of the sagacity and caution of the true Yankee husbandman. These qualities were fused in him and each became the sanction of the other.

In the long run, there is a world of difference between individualism on the spiritual plane and individualism on the economic plane. Were it not so, there would be no meaning in the phrase, "Stone walls do not a prison make," there would be no meaning in Christianity. And therein consists the beauty and the permanence of Emersonianism. For as the scope of practical enterprise and self-reliance becomes with every generation more limited, as the generality of men are caught with both feet in the net of economic necessity, and are led thereby to seek scope for their initiative in disinterested activity, just so the Emersonian doctrine comes into its own, the Emersonian virtues mount upward and create a self-reliance in the spirit itself. Emersonianism, in short, can only begin to be itself when it has taken its final place on the plane of poetry. In the nineteenth century, it was economic as well; it was the voice of just those forces which moved, enlarged, created the American scene; it corresponded to a real freedom of movement and opportunity;

pioneers, inventors, men of business, engineers, seekers of adventure found themselves expressed and justified in it. Emerson presided over and gave its tone to this world of infinite social fragmentation and unlimited free will, a world in which, as the presupposition was, everyone started fresh, as if dropped from the sky, where entanglements of heredity and disposition, foreclosures of opportunity, desires and aims that require an already fertilized field for their development, where the whole welter of human history and social complexity had not yet as it were obscured the morning of time.

In all this, Emerson was essentially passive. He was the child of his age, and he gave his Yankee instincts free play under the sanction of his Transcendental idealism. He never dreamed of moulding society, and he was incapable of an effective social ideal. Compare him in this respect with Carlyle. The social ideal of Carlyle was the Hero, and what Carlyle meant by the Hero was a particular kind of being whom all Englishmen understand: a creature of flesh and blood who leads men. No doubt, Carlyle was absurd enough; but what made him nevertheless a mighty man was that he had the faculty of devising and making intensely real and contagious a social ideal the rudiments of which actually existed in the people he was addressing. The English admire heroism; Carlyle made the Hero a palpable objective, and his countrymen were stirred through and through. Carlyle counts his disciples from generation to generation; strong men and leaders of men, they go out conquering and ruling creation, and there is hardly a British governor who does not feel upon his head the apostolic hands of Carlyle. Preposterous no doubt they are, having so little of the science and humility that are proper to our late-sprung arboreal species. But who will deny that the doctrine itself has served to make them good human material—for a better use?

What can Emerson show as a social ideal? *Representative Men.* Emerson has chosen six names, five of which are the names of writers, the sixth that of a man of action, Napoleon, whom, let us hope, Young America will not too closely emulate. The social ideal of Emerson, as Froude pointed out, is a sort of composite of the philosopher, the mystic, the skeptic, the poet, the writer and the man of the world. I wonder what passed through the mind of the American business man of Emerson's day when he heard all these phrases, phrases so unrelated to the springs of action within himself? Did he feel that his profound instincts had been touched and unified, did he see opening before him the line of a disinterested career, lighted up by a sudden dramatization of his own finest latent possibilities? Did he not rather, with a degree of reason, say to himself: "These papers will serve very well to improve my mind. I shall read them when I have the time"? And did he not thereupon set to work accumulating all the more dollars in order that he might have the more time to cultivate his mind—in legal phrase—after the event?

Looked at from this side, Emerson has all the qualities of the typical baccalaureate sermon; and the baccalaureate sermon, as we know, beautiful as it often is, has never been found inconveniently inconsistent with the facts and requirements of business life. A glance at Young America after so many generations of being talked to might well convince one that something is wrong with the baccalaureate sermon. Since the day of Emerson's address on "The American Scholar," the whole of American literature has had the semblance of one vast, all-embracing baccalaureate sermon, addressed to the private virtues of young men. It has been one shining deluge of righteousness, purity, practical mysticism, and at the end of ninety years the highest ambition of Young America is to be—do I exaggerate?—the owner of a shoe-factory. As a result of this exclusive approach through the personal conscience (a conscience by no means connected with disinterested ends and the real development of personality), society in America has stood for two things: in its private aspect as an immense preserve for the exercise of personal virtues like thrift and self-assertion; in its public aspect as a thing to be coddled with rich gifts (Philanthropy) or scrubbed back to the political intentions of 1776 (Reform).

Emerson is the patron saint of every one of these diverse, chaotic impulses—the gentle, chime-like Emerson who in days to come will sound and shine over a better world.

VII

But since I have spoken of the disciples of Carlyle as arguing the force, if not the validity, of his social ideal, I must add something about the disciples of Emerson, and the personal and social effects of Transcendentalism in American society.

George William Curtis I take to have been the typical Emersonian young man, and I am probably the only person of this generation who has read all his writings. This was the result of having rented a furnished house in California, very new and clean, with little idealistic mottoes hanging from every bracket. Great care had been given to the selection of artistic doorknobs and grass-plaited mats; the cupboards were stuffed with albums of wild-flowers and with notebooks filled with nature poems of the minor sort and pencilled observations always unfinished and in a vague, wavering hand. An aroma of delicate futility spread from this house, and while gradually becoming conscious of this, I discovered everywhere, on the shelves, in the closets, under the albums, the works of George William Curtis: lives, letters, essays, eulogies, orations. He was plainly the favourite author of the previous occupants, and wherever one sat down for a moment, there was George William Curtis at one's elbow.

A dozen or so types exhaust the range of a people, and I have known several duplicates of our milder American Addison. In action he was admirable as a driver-out of money-changers—the virginal candour of his type assured that. But he had that pale, earnest cast of mind which always comes from thinking more about what Sir Galahad did not do than about the object of his quest; and in fact the philosophy of George William Curtis is the most mournful exhibition I know of the inner workings of the reformer's mind. It is in his social criticism that he betrays the incurable boyishness, the superannuated boyishness of the Emersonian tradition in its main line of influence, and the quantity and quality of his understanding of society is fairly well summed up in his energetic though perfectly well-mannered invective against smoking cigarettes in the presence of ladies.

If Transcendentalism ran to seed in George William Curtis, what were its personal and social effects at the source? He would be an ungentle soul who did not feel a certain tenderness for the Brook Farmers, who did not wish that a really wicked world had been provided expressly for them to make over. New England was not wicked: it was only a very just expression of the Yankee temperament, and the reformers showed no disposition whatever to de-Yankeeize themselves. Their instincts were perfectly right; they rebelled against the sordidness of a world given over to economic self-assertion; but they did not recognize that in their day economic self-assertion was the law of the tribe, and that under those conditions the prettiest communism imaginable could be nothing better than group-assertion or moonshine. They approached society through the abstract impulsion of German and French philosophy; having received this impulsion, and being practical themselves, they had to "do something," and what they did was Brook Farm. Abolition was the one strictly social cause they supported, and the South had reason to know how abstract was the New England prosecution of that cause. Half the grotesque, pathetic and charming futility of men like Bronson Alcott is due to the extraordinary amount of intellectual and moral machinery they set running, without real pressure and without real purpose. They were like high-minded weathercocks on a windless day.

What is the moral of all this? It is the moral of all unattached idealism: that only as one can feel, deeply and organically, the pressure of society, can one feel, can one *become* oneself, fruitfully and deeply.

VIII

This moral is re-enforced quite specially by the case of James Russell Lowell.

Very little, it seems to me, is left of Lowell except the size of him. He was a sizable man, he remains a sizable figure, but one that has curiously gone blank. He occupied a considerable space in the world, he became that interesting psychological fact, a "standard poet," he has been used by the American people to stop the gap where a great critic ought to have been. What is wrong with him, what is missing in him, what has happened to him?

No American writer appears to have been more naturally gifted than Lowell. In his youth, he was all animal spirits and impressionability, a sunny, easy nature with a local tang at bottom that gave edge to an otherwise too mellifluous talent. He rose easily and at once out of the provincial atmosphere that constrained so many of his contemporaries. The Transcendentalists, having sprung from Calvinism, were unable to approach art unless they could in some way justify themselves by making it an organ of religion; they sanctified it by placing it at arm's length and rendering it abstract. Lowell was born without scruples of this kind; he read and wrote in a natural secular spirit, and his poems range pleasantly over the ranges of other poets, without effort and without missionary zeal, in a substantial and cultivated way. His critical essays are of a similar nature: what distinguishes them is a quality that belongs to the better sort of criticism not in his own age but in the age preceding it, the quality that Hazlitt called gusto. But he called Shakespeare his master. Why is it that Shakespeare is never the master of originating minds? Plato may be, or Dante, or Tolstoy, or one's uncle, or the village postmaster, but not Shakespeare. Conceive the discomfort of Shakespeare living had any one proclaimed himself a disciple. The ten-millionth Hindu is a more inevitable master; and certainly any one who requires a lesson of

Shakespeare* comes away with nothing but grace and good humour.

Lowell's mental framework was on a large scale, and yet one persistently feels that the framework was not filled in. Superficially, he appears the most complete, the most perfectly fused American literary personality; in reality, he suffered more than any other from the want of a suitable background and is the most unfulfilled of all. That is because his culture is European without the corresponding pressure of the European mind. He was the contemporary of Matthew Arnold, of Ruskin, of Taine; in his representative character, in his vitality, he is of a stature equal to any of these; but where they have ideas and passions, he remains the genial ambassador. The truth is that Lowell had no ideas, or rather what he had were dummy ideas like democracy and patriotism, which in common usage mean little or nothing but which enable the mind to go round and round in a large kind of way without involving the difficult intellectual act of clinching something. He paid the penalty of detaching himself, in a measure, from the ethical idea, which alone in its various ramifications has been able to make the New England temperament an interesting one, by being unable to arrive at any other.

For this he was not by any means to blame. The individual responds to the pressure exerted upon him; his epoch, his race, his social background determine the character of this pressure. Ideas rarely exist, and when they exist they never come to fruition, except as representative of forces lying behind the individual

* "Was there ever an author of such emotional importance whose reaction against false conventions of life was such an absolute zero as his?" WILLIAM JAMES: *Letters*, II, 336.

which press and focus the individual and make him the mouthpiece of something greater, deeper, wider than himself. The real forces of American life during the nineteenth century were forces to which Lowell was not fitted to respond; they were individualistic, ethical and spiritual—they were, in a word, Emersonian. The strength of Emersonianism in its own time lay in its being a genuine response to an economic situation, an answering pressure, a justification of universally experienced needs and impulses. And what is true of Emerson is true of other writers in their kind and degree. Thoreau, for example, was a man of less native intellectual power than Lowell, but precisely because he was individualistic, because, inadequate as his background was, he was a natural response to it, his talent became intense, and that vivid little genius of his, that pungent and confined personality, remains a most positive possession. All American thought of any eminence (and most of no eminence) has had the nature of a private message; and we have scarcely produced an even second-rate publicist. For deep responds to deep.

Now, it is equally plain that Lowell was deficient in the typical traits of effective American thought as that he was naturally endowed with the traits of a social thinker. He had no interest either in his ego or in the cosmos; he was not at home in high latitudes, could not abide Shelley, philologizes over the loftier passages of Spenser, never speaks of Goethe without vaguely insinuating a grudge against him; he was not concerned in pointing morals. On the other hand, he had a gift for satire, a quite genuine scholarship, a definite good taste in literature as such (in distinction from the Emersonian view of literature as a reservoir of examples, morals, phrases, allusions with which to dress out one's own philosophy), a wide experience of men and manners.

These are two altogether distinct sets of qualities: the point is, that while the first set, which Lowell did not possess, arrived in Emerson and Thoreau at a quite eminent fulfillment, the second set, which Lowell did possess, were scarcely fulfilled at all. Emerson and Thoreau achieved their individualistic philosophy, and in that philosophy their individualistic traits were fused and intensified; but Lowell never achieved a social philosophy, and as a result his social traits were scattered and frittered away. His gift for satire was scarcely developed beyond the clever doggerel of *The Fable for Critics*, his wide experience of men and manners served only to make him personally gracious and attractive, his scholarship, instead of serving to unearth and elucidate large conceptions and general ideas, served merely to exhibit a thousand unassociated verbal ingenuities, his taste in literature found expression in a series of critical essays every one of which is a *cul-de-sac*, with twinkling lights all along the way, but leading no-whither and ending with itself.

One runs through his poems with a quite astounding sense of talent wasted, prettified, conventionalized for the want of animating issues. Give him an adequate issue, and one finds his whole manner changes. Witness the *Commemoration Ode*, witness *The Biglow Papers*. Slavery and the Mexican war receive in *The Biglow Papers*, it seems to me, just the right measure of literary attention; and this is a felicity which, in the light of his general exuberance, powers of expression, strength and solidity, makes one feel that he could have risen aptly to issues of a more strictly social type had they existed in his background.

The poems of Lowell, in fact, exhibit something which no other body of American poems exhibit, a constant sense of the want of worthy material, a constant suspension of the best faculties. He marks time, rhymes because the rhymes insist upon coming, because of a sheer exuberance that cannot be gainsaid, aware all the while that his words are far more than adequate to anything they actually convey. Of no other American poet is this true: certainly not of Whitman, who, on the contrary, labours for language equal to his idea, nor of Longfellow in his gentle complacency, nor of Whittier, whose narrow but real talent was precisely modulated to the two or three things he had to say, nor of Emerson, whose words are a chime, choice and serene. And Lowell, on the other hand, as constantly seems to be on the point of rising to great issues, to be waiting for them, to be as it were making bids for them. Whenever his heart is fully engaged in his work (which is not often), whenever his emotion is really vented, the quality of his mind is thoroughly social—denser and of wider scope than that of any other American poet save Whitman. What it almost entirely wants is intellectual structure, intellectual solidity, ideas. Consider, for example, *The Present Crisis*. The emotional effect of such a passage as that beginning "For Humanity sweeps onward—" is very nearly a magnificent effect: the emotion of almost any poetry written merely to further a cause (and virtually all American poetry which has any claim to the epithet "social" has been written to further a cause) is thin and shrill beside it; it *has* density, it *has* scope, it *has* some of the splendour which goes with anything massive that has found a voice. But when one tries to discover the intellectual structure of it, the ideas in it, when one enquires what Humanity is and what it is sweeping onward *to*, one finds that Lowell is as vague and flatulent as Bryant. No social pressure, no defined issues, no discipline lies behind him. He is simply being magnificently and generously emotional in a social and intellectual vacuum.

Now Tennyson is not a poet from whom one expects ideas; he is conspicuously, among English poets, one who shunned ideas, shunned issues of every kind, and would have avoided them altogether if he could. *Locksley Hall,* aside from its curiously antiquated sentiment, also contains a picture of the onward sweep of humanity. It has none of the social passion of Lowell's poem, it presents no sort of coherent vision; the ideas in it, like the ideas in *Maud* and *In Memoriam,* once one disentangles them from their poetical glamour, emerge merely as part of the general intellectual bric-à-brac of the Victorian age, owing little to the personal experience of Tennyson himself. But the ideas are there; if they are dim and confused, it is not because Tennyson was ignorant of them, but because he was on the whole not interested in them; he employs them, not for the sake of the ideas, but because he regarded his own poetical function as a representative function and had somehow, if he was to make his particular faith prevail, to make it prevail among these ideas and over them. He was surrounded on all sides by men like Darwin, Mill, Carlyle, Newman, pressed on all sides by conflicting ideas and issues, and, with no native inclination for it, he was forced into the position of a fighter.

Such is the effect of a social background upon a writer with no native capacity for being a social force. Such is the effect of the want of a social background upon a writer with great native capacity for being a social force. For if the background of Lowell was, in its individual aspect, a spectacle of enterprise and pluck, socially it was arbitrary, bare and trivial. And there is no doubt that if Lowell had been produced by any European people he would have been a great man. Bred in New England, he was like a born general whose country persists in remaining at peace: such a man skirmishes about in his youth, picks petty quarrels, adopts a commanding attitude, thinks in regiments, and gradually settles down a little fatuously among other military men, talks tactics, tells war stories, reads the reminiscences of dead soldiers and writes negligible books on armament. In Europe, where the warfare of ideas, of social philosophies, is always an instant close-pressed warfare in which everyone is engaged, Lowell would have had the opportunity to bring his artillery into play. In America, where no warfare of ideas has ever existed, where ideas have always been acutely individual and ethical, and where public and social affairs, disjointed and vague, have always met with the yawning indifference that springs from a relative want of pressure behind, he inevitably became indifferent. His was the indifference of a simple and confirmed man of letters—that is to say, a poet who has made his peace with the world.

Lowell, in a word, never arrived at a comprehensive attitude towards the inner forces of which books, men and affairs are symptomatic. Now, a point of view in criticism, criticism in the genuine sense, is a working plan, a definition of issues, which at once renders it impossible to make one's peace with the world, at once and permanently sets one at odds with the world, inevitably makes the critic a champion and a man of war. Generous impulses and enthusiasms, which Lowell had abundantly in his youth, are not enough, unless they are re-enforced and in a way solidified into some sort of personal programme; the sort of programme which, to take instances from among Lowell's contemporaries,

Carlyle had in his hero-worship, Ruskin in his central idea of the interaction of harmonious art and harmonious life, Mazzini in his brotherhood of peoples, Taine in his theory of the *milieu*, Nietzsche in his supermorality. To have such a programme is not a limitation; it corresponds on the plane of ideas to style on the plane of letters. It is not merely the mark of intense individuality, not merely the trait which makes men significant and interesting: it is the condition of life in the intellectual and moral world.

III. THE PRECIPITANT

I

I HAVE been trying to show in what way a survey of American literature would inevitably lead us to certain general facts about American life. I opened the survey with a statement which I think no one will contradict, that in American literature something has always been wanting, that a certain density, weight and richness, a certain poignancy, a "something far more deeply interfused," simply is not there. Beginning with this clue and reaching an axiom to which it seemed to me to lead, I suggested a certain practical conclusion as the result of our enquiry: that those of our writers who have possessed a vivid personal talent have been paralyzed by the want of a social background, while those who have possessed a vivid social talent have been equally unable to develop their personalities.

There is, I think, something in some not very vague way unsatisfactory about each of the writers we have been examining. Taken as a whole, the most characteristic fact about them is a certain delicacy which arrives in literature almost in the degree to which it stands remote from life, achieves its own salvation (after the Puritan fashion) by avoiding contact with actuality. Almost all the greater American writers, placed beside their English contemporaries, have a certain all too unworldly refinement. Purity of style and delicacy of touch at once distinguish Emerson from Carlyle, and Hawthorne from any Victorian novelist; but the abyss between their writings and the world in which they lived is immeasurably greater. The American character speaks through them, of course, but it is the American character only in its most sublimated form, carefully cleansed as it were and highly rarefied. Nothing is more marked than their disinclination to take a plunge, reckless and complete, as Carlyle and Dickens did, into the rudest and grossest actualities. The poet Camoens on his deathbed observed that his life had been spent in trying to keep himself afloat in a stormy sea, and his only care had been to exercise his left hand with double energy so that his right hand might be free to hold his *Lusiads* aloft, uncontaminated by the waves. This is the whole story of American literature: in a more than usually difficult and sordid world, it has applied its principal energies to being uncontaminated itself. It has held aloof, as a consciously better part, like all American idealism. The talent is there, high and dry; and if it is not always too high, it is very often a great deal too dry.

In fact, we have in America two publics, the cultivated public and the business public, the public of theory and the public of activity, the public that reads Maeterlinck* and the public that accumulates money: the one largely feminine, the other largely masculine. Wholly incompatible in their ideals, they still pull together, as the ass and the ox must. But the ass shows

*1915.

no disposition to convert the ox, nor the ox the ass. They do not mitigate one another; they are, in biological phrase, infertile with one another.

But it happens that we have the rudiments of a middle tradition, a tradition that effectively combines theory and action, a tradition that is just as fundamentally American as either flag-waving or money-grabbing, one that is visibly growing but which has already been grossly abused; and this is the tradition that begins with Walt Whitman. The real significance of Whitman is that he, for the first time, gave us the sense of something organic in American life.

Whitman was himself a great vegetable of a man, all of a piece in roots, flavour, substantiality and succulence, well-ripened in the common sunshine. In him the hitherto incompatible extremes of the American temperament were fused. The refinement of the Puritan tradition, summed up as an original type in Jonathan Edwards, able to make nothing of a life so rude in its actuality, turned for its outlet to a disembodied world, the shadow-world of Emerson, Hawthorne and Poe, a world fastidiously intellectual in which only two colours exist, white and black. Whitman was the Antæus of this tradition who touched earth with it and gave it hands and feet. For having all the ideas of New England, being himself saturated with Emersonianism, he came up from the other side with everything New England did not possess: quantities of rude feeling and a faculty of gathering humane experience almost as great as that of the hero of the Odyssey. Living habitually among world ideas, world emotions, world impulses, and having experienced life on a truly grand scale, this extraordinary person, innocent as a pioneer of what is called urbanity, became nevertheless a man of the world in a sense in which ambassadors are not; and there is every reason to suppose that he would have been perfectly at home in the company of Achilles, or Erasmus, or Louis XIV.

This fact is full of meaning, and if any one doubts it let him dwell on the following record in *Specimen Days*. Whitman is describing what he did in the military hospitals at Washington during the war:

> For reading I generally have some old pictorial magazines or story papers—they are always acceptable. . . . In these wards, or on the field, as I thus continue to go round, I have come to adapt myself to each emergency, after its kind or call, however trivial, however solemn, every one justified and made real under its circumstances—not only visits and cheering talk and little gifts—not only washing and dressing wounds . . . but passages from the Bible, expounding them, . . . etc. (I think I see my friends smiling at this confession, but I was never more in earnest in my life.) In camp and elsewhere, I was in the habit of reading or giving recitations to the men. They were very fond of it, and liked declamatory pieces. We would gather in a large group by ourselves after supper, and spend the time in such readings, or in talking, and occasionally by an amusing game called the game of twenty questions.

This passage will serve very well to mark the distinction between Whitman and all the other American men of letters of his time. Could Emerson have recited "declamatory pieces," even if it was at the moment the one thing to do? Could Bryant have led a game of twenty questions? Could Edgar Allan Poe have expounded the Bible? Could Whittier have juggled with oranges? Could Lowell have pointed out the felicities that lurk in the pictorial adventures of Nick Carter and the Wharf Rats? Could any one of them, in short, have entered so fully and many-sidedly into the spirit of a great human situation? But allowing for certain inevitable differences in the *milieu* (orange-juggling and the adventures of Nick Carter being peculiarly democratic and modern), I am sure that Achilles, or Erasmus, or Louis XIV could have done so; and this is why I have called Whitman a man of the world.

It was in these ways that he gained his experience, in these ways that he shared it. And it is the more remarkable since he had sprung from the most provincial, inadaptable, homespun stock, his aspect being, as Edmund Gosse remembered it, like that of a plain old deal table, scrubbed and scrubbed and scrubbed. He let in the air of a wider world on those inadequate decencies; he came home to his own traditions like a prodigal son, visiting for a while, mingling an element of indulgent pity in his new sense of the limited old ways, aware of a few confidences that could not be shared any more and of so many things, human too, which could find no place there. To compare the particular homeliness of Whitman with the homeliness, for example, of *Snow-Bound* is at once to recall his line, "There was a child went forth."

And he challenged the abnormal dignity of American letters. The dignity of letters! No doubt in the perennial indignity of our world a considerable emphasis on that becomes all too easily the price of self-preservation. The possession of culture with us has always been rather a jealous possession, it has the nature of a right that has been earned, an investment that might have been a yacht, a country-house, or a collection of Rembrandts instead.

All this was especially true of the New York men of letters who formed the background of Whitman: Stedman, Stoddard, and their group, who cared so much for style, and for whom the essence of literature lay in its remoteness from Wall Street. They had the temperament of collectors and connoisseurs; and Whitman came in upon them thundering and with his coat off, like an inconvenient country uncle, puddling their artistic expectations. Could anything have been more disconcerting than his Olympian summary of what he calls the "endless supply of small coin . . . the dandies and ennuyées who flood us with their thin sentiment of parlours, parasols, piano-songs, tinkling rhymes, the five-hundredth importation—or whimpering and crying about something, chasing one aborted conceit after another," when, faced with this, he dwells only on a certain substantial grandeur in the mountains of white paper and the crashing presses that turn them out?

Whitman—how else can I express it?—precipitated the American character. All those things that had been separate, self-sufficient, incoördinate—action, theory, idealism, business—he cast into a crucible; and they emerged, harmonious and molten, in a fresh democratic ideal, based upon the whole personality. Every strong personal impulse, every coöperating and unifying impulse, everything that enriches the social background, everything that enriches the individual, everything that impels and clarifies in the modern world owes something to Whitman. And especially of those American writers who have written preëminently for young men—and which has not?—Whitman alone, it seems to me, has pitched his tone to the real spring of action in them.

All this indicates a function quite different from that of a poet in any but the most radical and primitive sense of the word (the sense in which it was held by Whitman himself), a man, that is to say, who first gives to a nation a certain focal centre in the consciousness of its own character. Virgil did this, Mazzini did this, Björnson did this; and it was the main work of Whitman to make fast what he called "the idea and fact of American Totality," an idea and fact summed up with singular completeness in his own character and way of life. Emerson before him had provided a kind of skeleton outline; but what Emerson drew in black and white Whitman filled in with colour and set in three dimensions.

A *focal centre*—that is the first requisite of a great people. And by this I do not mean the sense of national or imperial destiny which has consolidated the great temporal powers of history. I mean that national "point of rest," to adopt a phrase in which Coleridge indicated that upon which the harmony of a work of art is founded and to which everything in the composition is more or less unconsciously referred; that secure and unobtrusive element of national character, taken for granted, and providing a certain underlying coherence and background of mutual understanding which Rome, for example, had in everything the name of Cato called up, or England in her great remembered worthies, or the elder Germany in Martin Luther. "National culture," to speak in the dialect of our own time, is only the perhaps too-conscious equivalent of this element in which everything admirably characteristic of a people sums itself up, which creates everywhere a kind of spiritual team-work, which radiates outward and articulates the entire living fabric of a race.

For us, it seems to me, Whitman laid the cornerstone of a national ideal capable in this way of releasing personality and of retrieving for our civilization, originally deficient in the richer juices of human nature, and still further bled and flattened out by the "machine process," the only sort of "place in the sun" that is really worth having.

But at this point one has to discriminate. The social ideal of Whitman is essentially a collection of raw materials, molten and malleable, which take shape only in an emotional form. This emotional attitude is at bottom the attitude of a perfectly free personality, naturally affirmative, naturally creative; the rude material of right personal instinct, which is, however, antecedent to the direction personality is to adopt and to the ideas that are to inform it.

To ignore this distinction, as most of the direct disciples of Whitman have done, is to go wrong utterly. And in fact Whitman himself ignored the distinction, and himself went wrong. Perfectly right in all his instincts, perfectly right so long as he kept to the plane of instinct, he was lost on the plane of ideas. He lacked a sure sense of his own province and limitations. Influenced no doubt by his disciples, he began in later years to assume functions not properly his own, and the greatness and sweetness of his character were increasingly marred by much pomposity and fatuousness. He was led to speak not as a poet but as an authority, the painful results of which may be seen in his newspaper interviews.

All this was probably inevitable. Whitman's instinct was to affirm everything, to accept everything, to relish the personal and human elements in everything. For himself he accepted "sustenance, clothing, shelter and continuity." As regards the world, he was equally catholic and passive. Soldiers being the strapping upright animals they are, he accepts armies because armies breed them. He enjoys an old restaurateur because he knows how to select champagne, likes to look at nursemaids because they are so trim and wholesome and at fashionable women because they are so pretty and gay, likes money because of a certain strength it implies and business because it is so active, nimble and adventurous. On the plane of instinct, where he properly belongs, he is right in each case: on the plane of ideas, the practical effect is that, in accepting everything, he accepts the confusion of things and the *fait accompli*.

It is, in fact, the simple corollary of his thoroughgoing mood of affirmation on the personal, instinctive, emotional plane, that his ideas should be perfectly conventional. In ideas he is just an old-fashioned Jacksonian democrat. Except for a certain amount of uncommonly vigorous criticism, of the stock type, on American abuses, he never questions the old institutions. He takes for granted "the unform'd and nebulous state of many things, not yet permanently settled, but agreed on all hands to be the preparations of an infinitely greater future." He talks the greatest amount of nonsense about the "feudalism" of a contemporary Europe whose typical artists have been men like Tolstoy, Dostoevski, Millet, Thomas Hardy. He is never able to release himself from the vicious comparative; he is morbid about geography. Not being satisfied by the greatness of anything as a positive fact, he has to prove its greatness by belittling something else. A fertile plain strikes him at once as more fertile than any other plain on earth, a grand scene "outvies all the historic places of note," an American general is more of a general than Napoleon, an American poem has to be better than any poem hitherto.

All this is just what Bryant used to say—it is just our fun. And the funniest thing of all, from this point of view, is to find Whitman solemnly posed, as he records it, before a vast canvas twenty feet by twelve, representing "Custer's Last Rally," the work of one John Mulvany; finding its "physiognomy realistic and Western," with an "almost entire absence of the stock traits of European war pictures," and recommending that it be sent to Paris "to show Messieur Crapeau [*sic*] that some things can be done in America as well as others." A scene that demonstrates once for all that Whitman was never intended to be an authority, even on democracy.

An opportunity, and in certain respects also a faculty, Whitman had, in his own time and place, very similar to those of Montaigne. I mean by this, on the one hand, a malleable and still incoherent race to be interpreted to itself, to be articulated, to be brought into focus, and on the other a temperament typical of that race, a range of sympathy coincidental with it, and a power of revealing and in a sense fixing the racial norm. "I look within myself, I am only concerned with myself, I reflect on myself, I examine myself, I take pleasure in myself," said Montaigne; and all France for the first time saw itself in a looking-glass and fell together in a common discipline.

The raw materials of a racial norm Whitman provided; but—and in this he resembled Emerson—he was too passive to go further. He assembled in himself and his writings the characteristics of America—with him originated the most contagious, the most liberating, the most unifying of native impulses; but he failed to react upon them, to mould them, and to drive them home. He had no ideas, and he was satisfied to have none. He lacked, above all, intensity. He was too complacent. He was incapable of discipline and he did not see that discipline is, for Americans, the condition of all forward movement.

But the conventionality of Whitman's intellectual

equipment is not, for us, a necessary part of the personal attitude which he originated. History is filled with instances of men who, having been called upon to originate fresh points of view, have had, in order to establish these points of view, to adopt a severely conventional position towards most of the phenomena of their time. Each of these men has had his disciples in the letter and his disciples in the spirit—Martin Luther, for example, especially in questions economic and social. The direct and immediate children of Luther, those who have laid apostolic hands on one another from generation to generation, are simply the bourgeoisie of the world; but the true Lutherans are those who, in every age, have thought keenly and honestly and independently and have, in so doing, contributed stone by stone to the great catholicism of the future. So also with Whitman and the children of Whitman. It was inevitable, in the America of his time, that he should have been so much of an outrageous egoist (consider the provocation!), inevitable that he should, in Emerson's phrase, have swallowed the universe like a cake, inevitable that he should have been undiscriminating, confused and a little fatuous. To affirm sufficiently, he had to affirm everything.

We are in a different position, and we have different responsibilities. On the philosophical side, the simple doctrine of evolution, in its crude form the last word in Whitman's cosmos, has been refined and ripened. Above all, we have no excuse not to see that affirmation, in the most real sense, proceeds to a certain extent through rejection, by merely dropping off most of the old clothes that Whitman found quite good enough. To keep these old clothes, to affirm that since everything is good they must be good also, to embroider them and make them over and stalk about in them, loudly affirming one's own ego and the indiscriminate grandeur of all creation, with particular reference to the Whole Crowd of Good Americans—all this is not to continue and to reaffirm the right Whitmanian tradition; but it is, in a way, to have the sanction of Whitman's own character and experience, and it is, above all, to do what the typical contemporary Whitmanian does.

In some way—and primarily by returning upon Whitman as Whitman returned upon Emerson, not, as in that case, by adding emotion to intellect, but by adding intellect to emotion—the social ideal the raw materials of which have been provided by Whitman must be formulated and driven home.

II

The Whitmanians, meanwhile, have made haste to formulate out of these materials a certain number of spurious social ideals, the more dangerous the more plausible, and even the more "American," they are. One of these, and perhaps the most typical, is that of the "inspired millionaire," which has had such a vogue during these later years, and which, for all its tincture of "privilege," has many of the traits of Whitmanism. Just as Carlyle's Hero may be taken as a projection of what the typical Englishman seems to aspire to be, a sort of Lord Cromer with a halo, just as Nietzsche's Superman is a projection of what the typical modern German long struggled to be, a sort of Bismarck with a halo, so the "inspired millionaire" is a projection of what the typical American apparently struggles to be, a sort of Henry Ford with a halo. It is the type towards which the personal forces of the generality of Americans appear to be directed, heightened and justified as an ideal.

The notion of the "inspired millionaire" seems thus to have a certain validity. Indeed, the idealization of business has, in America, a certain validity which elsewhere it could not have. For business in America is not merely more engaging than elsewhere, it is even perhaps the most engaging activity in American life. One cannot compare the American commercial type with the commercial type that England has evolved without feeling in the latter a certain fatty degeneration, a solemn, sanctified, legalized self-satisfaction, which our agile, free, open, though sometimes indefinitely more unholy type is quite without; for even in his unholiness the unholy business man in America is engagingly crooked rather than ponderously corrupt. Beside the English business man, as one figures him at those Guildhall banquets which array themselves like a Chinese wall of beef against every impulse in life that moves and breathes, beside the English business man as he is apotheosized in the Lord Mayor of London (led by that symbolic coachman of his as a winged victory), with his chains and decorations, the liveries that fortify him, the legalities and charters that sanction him, the immemorial precedents that fix him foursquare and firm in his encumbered world—beside him, the American business man is a gay, sprightly, child-like being, moved and movable, the player of a game, a sportsman essentially, though with a frequently dim perception of the rules. One has only to compare the Bank of England, that squat impregnable mass which grips a score of London acres, with, for example, the Woolworth Tower, which has in it so much of the impulse that has built cathedrals, to feel this divergence in the quality of English and American business.

What is the natural history of this divergence? Why, precisely that the world of trade in England has always been an underworld, precisely that everything which is light, gay, disinterested, personal, artistic has held aloof from it, has been able to form a self-subsisting world that lies beyond it, while trade itself is only a dull residuum. The cream has risen to the top, and the world of business is perfectly conscious that it is only skimmed milk; and if the aldermen wax fat it is in a spirit that Americans would call defiance and despair. For in America there has been no such separation of the cream and the milk. Business has traditionally absorbed the best elements of the American character, it has been cowed by no sense of subjection, it has thriven in a free air, it has received all the leaven, it has occupied the centre of the field. Just those elements which in other countries produce art and literature, formulate the ideals and methods of philosophy and sociology, think and act for those disinterested ends which make up the meaning of life; just that free, disinterested, athletic sense of play which is precisely the same in dialectic, in art, in religion, in sociology, in sport—just these, relatively speaking, have in America been absorbed in trade. It is not remarkable that, on the one hand, our thought and literature are so perfunctory, while, on the other, American business is so seductive, so charming, so gay an adventure—not remarkable, for instance, that a recent writer is really able to imagine "a million dollars having a good time, i.e., a million dollars full of creative imagination."

Yet though trade may have all the grace and charm of sportsmanship, and all the fervour of a religion, though it may express itself in the most beautiful buildings, though it may stimulate the imagination, though it may turn a factory into an earthly paradise, can it really have the essential quality of religion, sport and art, can it be at bottom, that is to say, disinterested? So long as the impulse which underlies trade is not that of an exchange of equivalent values, but of an exchange that gets more than it gives and gets as much more as it can, just so long trade cannot be disinterested, and the problem of private subsistence in trade is inevitably bound up with the problem of arbitrary self-interest all the way up and down the scale. The ideal of the "inspired millionaire" is that of a disinterested man, a notion that plainly contradicts itself. For although a man may be disinterested after he has become a millionaire, it is quite impossible, except through inheritance (which is outside the present question), to be disinterested during the process of becoming one.

That is why the ideal of the "inspired millionaire" differs from the Superman and the Hero. The fact that it flatters the ordinary business man does not of itself invalidate it. Carlyle flattered the English aristocracy of his day, and Nietzsche flattered the Bismarckians and little supermen of Germany. Every social ideal has formed itself out of the stuff of some nation, has grown up as the reflex of its dominant moral type, and has apparently justified the type on its lower levels. The real question with any social ideal is not whether it seems to be embodied and debased in any existing class, but whether or not it provides a possible moral programme for the individual, a way of looking at life, a point of view. One may find the Superman a very objectionable ideal, but one has to admit that the Superman's unmorality is itself a moral attitude, a moral programme, a point of view; one may find Carlyle's Hero a ludicrously unscientific ideal, but one has to admit that the Hero considered as the interpreter of a reality which lies behind phenomena constitutes a moral attitude, a moral programme, a point of view. Both are conceivable social ideals. Is the "inspired millionaire" a conceivable social ideal? Is there, as a recent writer says, "no difference between making a fortune and making a book or a picture"? The one reply is simply that millionairism is itself not a moral entity like heroism or superhumanity: it is a situation, and a situation moreover that is not the inevitable result of any kind of activity, even the activity of a genius for acquisition.

III

The ideal of the "inspired millionaire" seems to me, nevertheless, a landmark and a touchstone. For it is in the direct line of the American tradition, it is the climax of our old Transcendental individualism. It springs, like the flower of the century plant, right out of the apparent heart, right out of the apparent centre, of American society.

The *apparent* centre, I say, because, although business is plainly the centre of attraction, I think it could easily be shown so to be only through the want of such an animating motive as a genuine social ideal provides. For if, in the first place, millionairism is not a moral entity and the "inspired millionaire" is therefore not a conceivable social ideal, if moreover trade itself cannot be in essence a disinterested thing, only consider what is involved in the very plausibility of this ideal, in the sportsmanship, the fervour, the charm that actually exist in American business! Only consider the meaning of such a paradox as that the mind of a nation is given over, in a potentially disinterested mood, to an essentially self-interested activity! Only consider that the will-to-reform, negative as it is, has sprung spontaneously out of the welter of business itself! Only consider how much disinterestedness all this, at bottom, amounts to! Who can say what would happen in America if some direct and positive outlet, some outlet normal to the disinterested mood, as the will-to-reform is not, were provided for all this energy that has taken the wrong switch? Who can say what would happen if some one were to appear with a social ideal as concrete as this, and just as much an answer to the experience of the American people, only genuine, central, clear and true?

How much talent goes to waste because there is no criticism, no standard, no authority to trip it up and shake it and make it think! On the one hand, we have the unwillingness and the incapacity of the self-interested financialized brain to extend itself to general ideas; on the other, an undisciplined emotionality face to face with crowds, millionaires, prairies and skyscrapers—an open sea with plenty of wind for the great American balloon.

Now since in a matter that concerns so many good Americans (for one must agree that most of the really first-rate forces in America have been and still are absorbed in business), since in this matter, and in consequence of this fact, America is so palpably superior to England, perhaps it may be pointed out how in the matter of ideas, and especially in the half-unconscious machinery that makes ideas tell, England is equally superior to America—and why, as a result of this, the problem of England is in certain fundamental respects more hopeful than the problem of America. For certainly the main work of society is to build that garden in the cosmic wilderness, as T. H. Huxley (best and brightest of the Philistines) described it; conceiving society deliberately as a work of art which is at war with nature, fertilizing the soil, cultivating and protecting the most beautiful and the greatest variety of plants, aware all the time that every moment we lay aside our tools or lose sight of our ever-developing design the weeds will pour back again and the wilderness will by so much have gained upon us.

The only education that can forward this plan is the education that teaches us what a weed is and what a flower is. And the only superiority which England has over America—a relative but a great superiority—is that England really has the rudiments of a sort of botanical laboratory of this kind. It has a few men who are skilled in recognizing weeds and in appreciating flowers and who are gradually building up a comprehensive design. While, just because (unlike political economists) they know they are dealing with human material, with an infinitely variegated and ever-changing material, they are far too sensible to confuse their study with an exact science, they have, I insist, most of the advantages of an exact science; that is to say, standing on a common level, they know where they are, their common rejections correspond roughly to rejections by evidence, they build on rejections, and they keep their spirits open towards the front. Having in mind the people as a whole, and every cross-section of the people (not merely the cross-section that has to do with them as "producers" or "consumers"), they feel each beat of the national pulse; they know what Methodism stands for, or the appearance of a new poet, or a Welsh festival, or an Irish Theatre, or a General Strike, or the statistics of unemployment, or a new book on political theory. This open, skeptical, sympathetic centrality of theirs articulates the whole life of the people, and incidentally as a matter of course expresses itself through legislation. More than one English book by an unknown writer has, within two years and owing to this diffused sense of the hierarchy of ideas, penetrated Parliament, convinced it, and been at once translated into action. Utopian event, which an innocent person might suppose the natural course of things in the most rudimentary legislature!

England, to be sure, is just as much the wilderness as America. All I am urging is that while England has at least a handful of trained gardeners, we have only cowboys and a flag.

IV. THE SARGASSO SEA

I

"THE fiddles are tuning as it were all over America." This is a remark of the best, the youngest and the most Irish of all good Americans, John Butler Yeats. It is true that under the glassy, brassy surface of American jocosity and business there is a pulp and a quick, and this pulpy quick, this nervous and acutely self-critical vitality, is in our day in a strange ferment. A fresh and more sensitive emotion seems to be running up and down the old Yankee backbone, that rarely blossoming stalk.

I am speaking myself as a thorough-going Yankee to other thorough-going Yankees—as a "little American" (to adopt a phrase which, as time goes on, may prove more and more useful). For to find this ferment in the immigrant folk of one, two or three generations is in itself only natural and the effect of a civilization, in their own past, that is, in certain ways, more vivid and more vital than our own. The importation of radical ideas and the ferment of radical ideas which have been imported scarcely touch, it seems to me, the centre of the American problem. So far as we are concerned, the sea-crossing, to begin with, has a very dampening effect on the gunpowder contained in them. Transplanted, they have at once the pleasing remoteness of literature and the stir of an only half-apprehended actuality; they become admirably safe, they become even delightful. In the American mind, Nietzsche and A. C. Benson—the lion and the lamb—lie down quite peacefully together, chewing the cud of culture. To get civilization out of the Yankee stock—*ex forte dulcitudo*—is the more arduous and the more inspiriting enterprise. Is it possible? Is it in process? The signs are anything but obvious: one has to keep quite still and hold one's ear close to the ground to hear the sap stirring and the little half-inconsequential voices that whisper and breathe in the intervals of bombast and business. For there is nothing so shy and so puzzled as the fine Puritan temperament face to face with a free world.

If something vibrates in the air, it is without doubt the expectation of a social ideal that shall act upon us as the sun acts upon a photographic plate, that shall work as a magnet upon all these energies which are on the point of being released. But the formulation of a social ideal can only be the work of a wiser head and a riper heart than we have yet seen; and we have had, meanwhile, quite enough of the egotism which, with foolish head and unripe heart, has undertaken this intoxicating function.

If it is for the State to weed out the incentives to private gain, it is for us meanwhile simultaneously to build up other incentives to replace them. These incentives must be personal. They must not spring from floating, evanescent ideals, political, spiritualistic or other; they must touch the primitive instincts that are touched by the incentives they replace. Emerson gave us the Over-Soul; Catholicism gave us the Madonna and the Bambino: which has really touched the religious sense of mankind?

II

America is like a vast Sargasso Sea—a prodigious welter of unconscious life, swept by ground-swells of half-conscious emotion. All manner of living things are drifting in it, phosphorescent, gayly coloured, gathered into knots and slotted masses, gelatinous, unformed, flimsy, tangled, rising and falling, floating and merging, here an immense distended belly, there a tiny rudimentary brain (the gross devouring the fine)—everywhere an unchecked, uncharted, unorganized vitality like that of the first chaos. It is a welter of life which has not been worked into an organism, into which fruitful values and standards of humane economy have not been introduced, innocent of those laws of social gravitation which, rightly understood and pursued with a keen faith, produce a fine temper in the human animal.

Now, as everybody knows, there was a time when the actual Sargasso Sea was, to the consciousness of science, just in this uncharted state. The creatures it contains, instead of being studied with reference to an organic unity of which they were all modifications, were divided into certain fixed sub-kingdoms according as they superficially resembled one another; here a group with soft bodies, there a group whose organs were disposed about a centre, and the like. It was, I think, T. H. Huxley who first exposed the superficiality of this method and who began the grouping of creatures according to real identity in structure.

American society, so to speak, is in this pre-

Darwinian state. It is filled with "groups" that have no real meaning, groups that do not stand for living issues, do not engage our personal energies. A Democrat is no more a genuine type than one of the pre-Darwinian Mollusca, so called because they had soft bodies; a Republican is no more a genuine type than one of the Radiata, so called because their organs were disposed about a centre. The superficial characteristics of the types remain—that is to say, Democrats generally *have* soft bodies, and Republicans *do* believe in centralization—but the fruitful elements of a group have departed from them. They no longer touch men's vital instincts.*

The recognized divisions of opinion, the recognized issues, the recognized causes in American society are extinct. And although Patriotism, Democracy, the Future, Liberty are still the undefined, unexamined, unapplied catchwords over which the generality of our public men dilate, enlarge themselves and float (exact and careful thought being still confined to the level of engineering, finance, advertising and trade)—while this remains true, every one feels that the issues represented by them are no longer genuine or adequate.

The most striking American spectacle today is a fumbling about after new issues which no one as yet has been able to throw into relief. We have seen one president advocating a "New Nationalism," another president advocating a "New Freedom," a well-known novelist talking about a "New Patriotism"—phrases that illustrate just this vague fumbling, this acute consciousness of the inadequacy of the habitual issues,

* "For a good many years past, there has been no real issue on which thinking Americans have divided into Democrats and Republicans."—President Eliot, 1913. Quoted in Henry James, *Charles W. Eliot*, II, 230.

this total inability to divine and formulate new issues that really are issues. With us the recognized way of pinning down something that is felt to be in the air is to adopt some cast-off phrase and tack the word "New" before it. A pleasant thrill then runs over the country, something which is vaguely felt to be new having been recognized and labelled as new, and the issue itself is quietly smothered.

The truth is that it signifies nothing for politicians to import social issues into the plane of politics, even if they import the whole of socialism into politics, so long as they and we fail to recognize that the centre of gravity in American affairs has shifted wholly from the plane of politics to the plane of psychology and morals. So long as we fail to recognize this, politics can only continue the old endless unfruitful seesaw of corruption and reform. That is why catchwords like the "New Nationalism" and the "New Freedom" are really so much further from the centre of gravity than catchwords like "Highbrow" and "Lowbrow," or "Bromide" and "Sulphite." The latter lead nowhither, but they at least explain things. "Are you a Bromide?" may be a silly question, but it is by no means a silly fact that a whole population should have gone about putting that question. It is a fact that grows in meaning when one considers that not so much as a remnant of the American people can go about *thinking* any question that stands for a social and psychological issue which cuts deeper than that.

It is pathetic, it is almost tragic. How much hunger is represented by all these "new" things that give the American public such a quantity of gas-and-water to stay their appetites? How much of a real psychological curiosity miscarries at the outset in questions like "Are you a Bromide?" American slang in general, alive with psychological interest in a rudimentary state, is the most mournful tribute to a vitality in the American people, missing fire in a million trivialities, because it has not been engaged by issues that really touch home in the sphere of personality, because—to put it the other way round—the catchwords, or the watchwords, of American society are not themselves personal.

For it may as well be understood that the human race will have catchwords and will not budge without them. Consequently, it makes all the difference to a people and an age whether its catchwords really do or do not correspond with convictions, and whether these convictions really do or do not reach down among the real problems of personal and social life—whether they really *catch* at the bottom of things, like a dredging-machine, or whether they merely scrape along the bottom or stir up the water or ruffle the surface. Home Rule, No Taxation without Representation, the Right of Private Judgment, the Three Unities are catchwords that have played an immense part in the world of thought and action, because they have stood for genuine causes, genuine issues in religion, in politics, in art. The rank and file who grasp the idea behind them incompletely and in varying degrees and who, if they depended on their understanding of the idea, would be at sixes and sevens, grasp the catchword and unite on a common platform which, if the catchword is a worthy one, educates them through action. Every leader will have his catchword: his philosophy will be a "Synthetic" philosophy, his ideal will be the "Superman," his *bête noire* will be the "Servile State," and the generality of men will fall in line according to whether the connotations of these catchwords do or do not come home to them. The test of a living society, a living philosophy or art, is whether or not the catchwords it flings forth really correspond with profound divisions of type, deeply felt issues, genuine convictions, in whichever field, between—I was going to say—some good and some evil. But these words are so unfashionable that if I use them I shall certainly alienate any Advanced Person who honours these pages with a glance.

But it makes no difference how many games of pea-and-thimble philosophy may play, wherever the thimble is put down the problem of good and evil is the pea that lies under it; and the happiest excitement in life is to be convinced that one is fighting for all one is worth on behalf of some clearly seen and deeply felt good and against some greatly scorned evil. To quicken and exhilarate the life of one's own people—as Heine and Nietzsche did in Germany, as Matthew Arnold, William Morris and H. G. Wells have done in England—is to bring, not peace, but a sword. With Heine the warfare was between philistinism and enlightenment, with Nietzsche between master-morality and slave-morality, with Matthew Arnold between Hebraism and Hellenism, with Morris between machinery and handicraft, with Wells between muddle-headedness and fine thinking. There are five distinct conceptions of good and five distinct conceptions of evil. And each of these pairs of opposed catchwords stands for a conceivable interpretation of society, a cleavage in things like the cleavage of the Red Sea. Accept them or not as one chooses, they go down so deep that one can walk dry-shod between them.

To this happy excitement of urgent issues is due the happy excitement of European thought, the muscular and earthy sense of opposition under which personality becomes aware of itself and grows with a certain richness. I do not know how much dull pain, poverty and chagrin are responsible for these manifestations of high pressure: but certainly it is a pressure of this kind that forces the European to define his position, to form his own microcosm, and by virtue of which the catchwords that correspond with issues defined really represent something and are apt, relatively speaking, to cut deep. And certain it is that, while European literature grows ever closer and denser and grapples to life more and more, American literature grows only windier and windier. One finds in Mr. Wells what seems at times as irresponsible a mysticism as that of any American. But while the American tendency is to begin in the air and remain in the air, one scarcely finds a European thinker who has not earned his right to fly by serving an apprenticeship with both feet on the ground: if he leaves the earth it is because he has been pressed from it, and he carries flesh and blood and clods of earth with him. One cannot have too much mysticism; but, on the other hand, one cannot have enough good human mud for ballast. The pressure which actuates the European mind is due no doubt to a vast deal of dull pain, poverty and chagrin. But are we Americans very much happier? In America, I think, pain, poverty and chagrin are at last as omnipresent as anywhere else, and so far we have devised no compensation for them.

Self-fulfillment is the immemorial compensation for having eaten of the fruit of good and evil, and under the conditions of modern life self-fulfillment has to be a somewhat artificial thing. In a world of instincts blunted by trade, system and machinery, the sweat of the brow, the resurgence of the seasons, the charm of perfect colour and of pure form are not for the generality of men sufficient. The exhilarating sense of conflict and of rest from conflict which together make up the meaning of life, no longer universally possible on the plane of instinct, have largely come to exist in the more contagious, the more gregarious world of the intelligence. In that world the majority are lost and astray unless the tune has been set for them, the key given them, the lever and the fulcrum put before them, the spring of their own personalities touched from the outside.

In the midst of the machine age, as everybody knows, it was the contagious personality of William Morris which opposed the ideal of craftsmanship to the ideal of cheapest work and largest money and substituted for the inhumane stimulus of competition the humane stimulus of fellowship. No doubt, this was only a drop in the bucket. But, speaking relatively, picture to yourself what might have been the inner mind even of the average artisan—to adopt the phrase of advertising—Before and After the William Morris treatment. One contagious personality, one clear shadowing forth of opposed issues—a good and an evil, a humane and an inhumane—touched the spring of personality in how many workingmen! and gave them how rich and how adequate a reason to turn over this world of ours, as a spade turns over a clod of earth. It is of no use to talk about Reform. Society will be very obedient when the myriad personalities that compose it have, and are aware that they have, an object in living.

How can one speak of progress in a people like our own that so sends up to heaven the stench of atrophied personality? How can one speak of progress in a people whose main object is to climb, peg by peg, up a ladder which leads to the impersonal ideal of private wealth? How can the workingman have any reality or honesty of outlook when he regards his class merely as an accidental, temporary group of potential capitalists? And the university man, the man, that is to say, who has had the fullest opportunity to seek and find a disinterested end in living, an end to which the machinery of self-preservation, however compelling, remains yet in subservience, the man who has within him a world of ineffectual dreams and impotent ideals—what has he to actuate him but a confused and moralized instinct that somehow he must make a lot of money?

It is not a question of blame. One cannot blame the individual, even as a citizen, though as a citizen he overtly upholds the conception of society which is responsible for his helplessness as an individual. His personality, his latent energies go to waste just as the personalities of so many artisans would have gone to waste if there had been no William Morris. The way has not been made straight for him, the waters of the sea of good and evil have not been divided for him; he flounders in the mud and the waves, until at last, if he is fortunate, he drowns in a million dollars. It is the economic individualist himself who blames people; socialism has the impersonal charity of science.

III

Issues that make the life of a society do not spring spontaneously out of the mass. They exist in it—a thousand potential currents and cross-currents; but they have to be discovered like principles of science, they have almost to be created like works of art. A people is like a ciphered parchment that has to be held up to the fire before its hidden significances come out. Once the divisions that have ripened in a people have been discerned and articulated, its beliefs and convictions are brought into play, the real evils that have been vaguely surmised spring into the light, the real strength of what is intelligent and sound becomes a measurable entity. To cleanse politics is of the least importance if the real forces of the people cannot be engaged in politics; and they cannot be so engaged while the issues behind politics remain inarticulate.

In spite of their frequent show of strength and boldness, no ideas in America are really strong or bold —not because the talents are wanting but because the talents and the mass have not been brought into conflict. No serious attempt has been made to bring about the necessary contraposition of forces, to divine them, to detach them, to throw them into relief; the real goats and the real sheep have not been set apart. There has not in fact been one thinker strong enough to create a resisting background in the vague element of American life.

To create this resisting background must be the first work of our thinkers. It is incomparably difficult, for it is like standing on clouds and attempting to gain purchase for a lever. The vast, vague movements of sentiment in the democracy directly produce the conventionality of our ideas, for there is no clinch in things, nothing to brace the feet against, no substance against which ideas can assume a bold relief. "To preserve the freedom of the will in such expansion," says Victor Hugo (who had reason to know), "is to be great"; and certainly the man who can throw American life into relief will be a man out of a hundred million.

But how shall we know him when he comes?—we who have invented the phrase "any old thing," we whose watchword has always been "just about as good," we who delight in plausible mediocrity and are always ready with tinkling cymbals to greet the sounding brass? To leave behind the old Yankee self-assertion and self-sufficiency, to work together, think together, feel together, to believe so fervently in the quality of standards that we delight in prostrating our work and our thoughts before them—all that is certainly in the right direction. "My belief becomes indefinitely more certain to me as soon as another shares it" is the true catholic observation of a German poet, which all good Americans ought to ponder; for intimate feeling, intimate intellectual contact, even humour—that rich, warm, robust and all-dissolving geniality which never, I think, quite reached the heart of Mark Twain—it is these we chiefly lack. These are the enemies of that base privateness which holds the string of what we call publicity. It is these that promote that right, free, disinterested publicity which the real gentleman, the real craftsman, the real civil servant has always had in his blood.

Socialism flows from this as light flows from the sun. And socialism is based on three facts that have great dignity—hunger, science and good will. Is it "against human nature"? The foolish socialist laughs in his sleeve when he hears this, convinced as he is that human nature is the sport of circumstance, and that when the time is right human nature will fall in line as the trees fall in line through the process of the seasons. Only the foolish socialist stops there. To be a sheer determinist is in all probability to have behind one the authority of the intellect. But human nature is an elusive magical thing which has the faculty of submitting its intellect to all manner of sea-changes. Determinism, which at one moment appears to enslave man, may at the next become the slave of man. There is a free will within determinism by which, as it were, men can cheat nature, convincing themselves—and with a whole heart—that what nature wills is what they will: and if they will it enough, which is master of the situation? We Americans ought to know, for we have produced one of the greatest of determinists, and one of the greatest of all transmuters of determinism:

My foot is tenoned and mortised in granite,
I laugh at what you call dissolution,
And I know the amplitude of time.

All forces have been steadily employed to complete and delight me;
Now on this spot I stand with my robust soul.

IV

All Americans are good—this to me is an axiom; but we are good as the Germans used to be a hundred years ago, as good, that is, as bread which is baked without yeast. We are good and we are humble. We have so schooled ourselves in humility that nobody in the world more carefully, more steadily (and more unjustly) takes down our pretensions than the educated American. In the end, perhaps, our humility will save us. But the acquisition of culture and the acquisition of money—"Highbrow" and "Lowbrow"—are equally impersonal, equally extraneous to the real matter, equally incapable of arousing the one thing needful. When the women of America have gathered together all the culture in the world, and the men have collected all the money—who knows?—perhaps the dry old Yankee stalk will begin to stir and send forth shoots and burst into a storm of blossoms. Strange things happen. I have heard of seeds which, either planted too deep or covered with accretions of rubble, have kept themselves alive for generations until by chance they have been turned up once more to the friendly sun. And, after all, humanity is older than Puritanism.

Letters and Leadership

1918

I. OLD AMERICA

I

THERE is a certain spot in New York where I often ruminate in the summer noontime, a lonely, sunny, windy plaza surrounded by ramshackle hoardings and warehouses unfinished and already half in ruin. It is the fag-end of a great cross-town thoroughfare, a far-thrown tentacle, as it were, of the immense monster one hears roaring not so far away, a tentacle that lies there sluggish and prone in the dust, overtaken by a sort of palsy. To the right and left stretches one of those interminable sun-swept avenues that flank the city on east and west, wide, silent and forsaken, perpetually vibrating in the blue haze that ascends from its hot cobblestones, bordered on one side by rickety wharves, on the other by a succession of tumbledown tenements left there like the sea-wrack at the ebb of the tide. For scarcely a living thing lingers here about the frayed edges of the town; it is as if one had been suddenly set down in the outskirts of some pioneer city on the plains of the Southwest, one of those half-built cities that sprawl out over the prairie, their long streets hectically alive in the centre but gradually shedding their population and the few poor trees that mitigate the sun's glare, till at last, all but obliterated in alkali dust, they lose themselves in the sand and the silence.

All our towns and cities, I think, have this family likeness and share this alternating aspect of life and death—New York as much as the merest concoction of corrugated iron and clapboards thrown together beside a Western railway to fulfil some fierce evanescent impulse of pioneering enterprise. Like a field given over to fireworks, they have their points of light and heat, a district, a street, a group of streets where excitement gathers and life is tense and everything spins and whirls; and round about lie heaps of ashes, burned-out frames, seared enclosures, abandoned machinery, and all the tokens of a prodigal and long-spent energy.

But it is the American village that most betrays the impulse of our civilization, a civilization that perpetually overreaches itself only to be obliged to surrender again and again to nature everything it has gained. How many thousand villages, frost-bitten, palsied, full of a morbid, bloodless death-in-life, villages that have lost, if they ever possessed, the secret of self-perpetuation, lie scattered across the continent! Even in California I used to find them on long cross-country walks, villages often enough not half a century old but in a state of essential decay. Communities that have come into being on the flood-tide of an enterprise too rapidly worked out, they all signify some lost cause of a material kind that has left humanity high and dry —like the neutral areas in an old painting where the colour, incompetently mixed and of perishable quality, has evaporated with time.

I suppose it is only natural in the West to find these decayed settlements where time has taken so seriously, as it were, mankind's contempt for permanence. What shocks one is to realize that our Eastern villages, the seats of all the civilization we have, are themselves scarcely anything but the waste and ashes of pioneering, and that no inner fire has taken possession of the hearth where that original flame so long since burned itself out.

Off and on during the summers I have stayed in one of those ancient Long Island villages that still seem to preserve a little of the atmosphere of the early Republic. The crazy, weather-beaten houses that hold themselves up among their unkempt acres with a kind of angular dignity, the rotting porches and the stench of decay that hangs about their walls, the weed-choked gardens, the insect-ridden fruit-trees, the rusty litter along the roads, the gaunt, silent farmers who stalk by in the dusk—how overwhelmingly they seem to betray a losing fight against the wilderness! For generations every man has gone his own way and sought his own luck. Nature has been robbed and despoiled and wasted for the sake of private and temporary gains, and now, having no more easy rewards to offer, it is taking its revenge on a race that has been too impatient and self-seeking to master its inner secrets. Incapable of coöperating with nature, of lying fallow, of merging itself, as it were, in the great current of life, this race has accumulated no buoyant fund of instinct and experience, and each generation, a little more spiritually impoverished than the last, runs out the ever-shortening tether of self-reliance. Still a race of pioneers, pioneers or nothing, it has lost the sap of adventure without developing beyond the stage of improvisation.

It is all so familiar, so intensely American, and yet the warm ancestral bond eludes one so! One looks out over a landscape everywhere abundant and propitious, but still in some way, after so many years of tillage, unimpregnated by human destiny, almost wholly wanting in that subtle fusion of natural and human elements which everywhere the European landscape suggests. For Europe is alive in all its members; in its loneliest and most isolated corner there is hardly a hamlet where life does not still persist, as green and warm and ruddy as the heart of an old olive-tree. Some profound inertia, some imperturbable tenacity of the spirit, has prevented it from quite surrendering to nature anything, a bit of ground, a house, a road, that has once passed into the keeping of the race. And thus, while the conquest has been laborious, while invention has been tardy, and means and ideas have been few and inadequate, something cumulative survives.

Old American things are old as nothing else anywhere in the world is old, old without majesty, old without mellowness, old without pathos, just shabby and bloodless and worn out. That is the feeling that comes over one in villages like this, capable only of being galvanized by some fresh current of enterprise into a semblance of animation. Inhabited as they have always been by a race that has never cultivated life for its own sake, a race that has lived and built and toiled always conscious of the possibility of a greater advantage to be found elsewhere, there is no principle of life working in them, three hundred years of effort having bred none of the indwelling spirit of continuity.

II

"Why is it," asks the author of *Jude the Obscure*, "that these preternaturally old boys always come out of new countries?" It was the spectacle of Jude himself, transplanted from Australia into the midst of the ancient peasantry of southern England, that prompted the question, and I remember with what force it came into my mind once, during a brief visit in Oxford, when, accustomed as my eyes for the moment were to the jocund aspect of young England in flannels, I came upon a company of Rhodes scholars from across the Atlantic. Pallid and wizened, little old men they seemed, rather stale and flat and dry; and I said to myself, it is a barren soil these men have sprung from —plainly they have never known a day of good growing weather. They might not have been typical Rhodes scholars, these men—I don't pretend to any wide knowledge of the species. But I know that, as often happens abroad when we encounter the things of home in unfamiliar surroundings, they brought to a head certain obscure impressions that had long been working in my imagination. I remembered, for instance, the "young instructors" I had encountered between Boston and San Francisco; I remembered the sad, sapless air of so many of them and their sepulchral voices, the notes of that essential priggishness the characteristic of which, according to Chesterton, is to have more pride in the possession of one's intellect than joy in the use of it. I fell to thinking about this professor and that I had known at home, and about our intellectual and artistic life in general. How anæmic it seemed, how thin, how deficient in the tang and buoyancy of youth, in personal conviction and impassioned fancy, how lacking in the richer notes! And at last there arose in my mind the memory of a concert at which half the accepted American composers had appeared on the stage one after another, grave, earnest, high-minded, and tinkled out their little intellectual harmonies. Surely, I said to myself again, there is something sadly amiss with our creative life.

Am I wrong in my impression that our "serious" people really are like leaves prematurely detached from the great tree of life? As a class they seem never to have been young, and they seem never to grow mellow and wise. Take our earnest popular novelists off guard; read their occasional comments on society, on the war, even on their own art. How dull, how mechanical, how utterly wanting in fresh insight their minds in general are! Mr. Winston Churchill, expatiating on citizenship, talks in one breath with all the puzzled gravity of a child and some of the weary flatulence of a retired evangelist. Even when they are not evangelical but writers merely they still seem somehow uprooted from the friendly soil. Something infinitely old and disillusioned peers out between the rays of George Ade's wit, and Mrs. Wharton's intellectuality positively freezes the fingers with which one turns her page. And it is the same in our other arts, the plastic arts alone perhaps excepted. Think of that one little vibrant chord, like a naked nerve perpetually harped on, that constitutes the theatrical art of Mrs. Fiske! Think of the arctic frigidity of Mr. Paul Elmer More's criticism! That little seed of the spirit a wayward and unlucky wind has planted in them, why has it never been able to take on flesh and blood, why has it so dried up the springs of animal impulse? It is as if, driven in upon themselves, their lives were a constant strain, as if their emotional natures had run dry and they had come to exist solely in their intellects and their nerves, as if in fact they had gone grey and bloodless precisely in the measure that an inflexible conscience had enabled them in spite of all to trim the little lamp that flickers in them.

Grow they certainly do not. With immense difficulty our intellectual types forge for themselves a point of view with which they confront the world, but like a suit of armour it permits no further expansion. They do not move easily within it; they are chafed and irritated by it; in order to breathe freely they are obliged to hold themselves rigidly to the posture they have at first adopted; and, far from being able to develop spontaneously beyond this original posture, they have to submit to its cramping limitations until the inevitable shrinkage of their mental tissues brings them release and relief.

Whatever the reason may be, it is certain that the long-fermented mind, the counsellor, the wise old man of letters, the mind that relates past, present and future, is a type our civilization all but utterly fails to produce. Our thinking class quickly reaches middle age, and, after a somewhat prolonged period during which it seems to be incapable of assimilating any fresh experiences, it begins to decay. The rest of our people meanwhile never even grow up. For if our old men of thought come to a standstill at middle age, our old men of action, as one sees them in offices, in the streets, in public positions, everywhere! are typically not old men at all but old boys. Greybeards of sixty or seventy, mentally and spiritually indistinguishable from their sons and grandsons, existing on a level of reflection and emotion in no way deeper or richer than that of their own childhood, they seem to have miraculously passed through life without undergoing any of life's maturing influences.

III

In short, I think we are driven to the conclusion that our life is, on all its levels, in a state of arrested development, that it has lost, if indeed it has ever possessed, the principle of growth.

To the general sense of this, many of the main documents in our recent literature bear witness. Consider, for example, those vast literary pyramids of Theodore Dreiser, those prodigious piles of language built of the commonest rubble and cohering, in the absence of any architectural design, by sheer virtue of their weight and size. Dreiser's Titans and Financiers and Geniuses are not even the approximations of men in a world of men—they are monsters, blindly effectuating themselves, or failing to effectuate themselves, in a primeval chaos; and the world wears them and wearies them as it wears and wearies the beasts of the field, leaving them as immature in age as it found them in youth. Cowperwood, the financier, put in prison as a result of his piratical machinations, weaves chair-bottoms and marks time spiritually against the day of his release, when he snaps back into his old self absolutely unaltered by reflection; and of Eugene Witla, after he has passed through seven hundred and thirty-four pages of soul-searing adventure, Dreiser is able to enquire: "Was he not changed then? Not much, no. Only hardened intellectually and emotionally, tempered for life and work." Puppets as they are of an insensate force which has never been transmuted into those finer initiatives that shed light on human destiny, they are insulated against human values; love and art pass into and out of their lives like things of so little meaning that any glimmer of material opportunity outshines them; and therefore they are able to speak to us only of the vacuity of life, telling us that human beings are as the flies of summer.

And then there is the *Spoon River Anthology*. The immense and legitimate vogue of this book is due to its unerring diagnosis of what we all recognize, when we are confronted with it, as the inner life of the typical American community when the criterion of humane values is brought to bear upon it in place of the criterion of material values with which we have traditionally pulled the wool over our eyes. It is quite likely, of course, that Masters, with a reasonable pessimism, has exaggerated the suicidal and murderous tendencies of the Spoon Riverites. But I know that he conveys an extraordinarily just and logical impression. He pictures a community of some thousands of souls every one of whom lives in a spiritual isolation as absolute as that of any lone farmer on the barren prairie, a community that has been utterly unable to spin any sort of spiritual fabric common to all, which has for so many generations cherished and cultivated its animosity towards all those non-utilitarian elements in the human heart that retard the successful pursuit of the main chance that it has reduced itself to a spiritual desert in which nothing humane is able to take root and grow at all. And yet all the types that shed glory on human kind have existed in that, as in every community! They have existed, or at least they have been born. They have put forth one green shoot only to wither and decay because all the moisture has evaporated out of the atmosphere that envelops them. Poets, painters, philosophers, men of science and religion, are all to be found, stunted, starved, thwarted, embittered, prevented from taking even the first step in self-development, in this amazing microcosm of our society, a society that stagnates for want of leadership, and at the same time, incurably suspicious of the very idea of leadership, saps away all those vital elements that produce the leader.

For that is the vicious circle in which we revolve. In the absence both of an intellectual tradition and a sympathetic soil, we who above all peoples need great men and great ideals have been unable to develop the latent greatness we possess and have lost an incalculable measure of greatness that has, in spite of all, succeeded in developing itself. For one thing, we have lost an army of gifted minds, of whom Henry James and Whistler are only the most notorious examples, minds about which our intellectual life could have rallied to its infinite advantage, as it always does when born leaders are in the field.

But the loss, great and continuing as it is, of so many talents that we have repelled and poured out, talents that have been driven to an exotic development in other countries, is really nothing beside what we have lost in ways that are perhaps less obvious. We are the victims of a systematic process of inverse selection so far as the civilizing elements in the American nature are concerned. Our ancestral faith in the individual and what he is able to accomplish (or, in modern parlance, to "put over") as the measure of all things has despoiled us of that instinctive human reverence for those divine reservoirs of collective experience, religion, science, art, philosophy, the self-subordinating service of which is almost the measure of the highest happiness. In consequence of this, our natural capacities have been dissipated; they have become ego-centric and socially centrifugal and they have hardened and become fixed in the most anomalous forms. The religious energy of the race, instead of being distilled and quintessentialized into the finer inspirations of human conduct, has escaped in a vast vapour that is known under a hundred names. So also our scientific energy has been diverted from the study of life to the immediacies of practical invention, our philosophy, quite forgetting that its function is to create values of life, has oscillated between a static idealism and a justification of all the anæmic tendencies of an anæmic age, and our art and literature, oblivious of the soul of man, have established themselves on a superficial and barren technique.

Of all this individualism is at once the cause and the result. For it has prevented the formation of a collective spiritual life in the absence of which the individual, having nothing greater than himself to subordinate himself to, is either driven into the blind alley of his appetites or rides some hobby of his own invention until it falls to pieces from sheer craziness. Think of the cranks we have produced!—not the mere anonymous cranks one meets, six to a block, in every American village, but the eminent cranks, and even the preëminent cranks, men who might so immensely more have enriched our heritage if we had been able to assimilate their minds, nurturing and disciplining them out of their aberrant individualism. For every member of the vast army of American cranks has been the graveyard of some "happy thought," some thought, happier than his neighbours have had, which has turned sour in his brain because the only world he has known has had no use for it. As for our literature, it is quite plain that there is nothing inherently "greater" in many of the writers whose work we import (and rightly import) from abroad than in writers of a corresponding order at home. The former simply have been able to make a better use of their talents owing to the complicated system of critical and traditional forces perpetually at play about them.

For only where art and thought and science organically share in the vital, essential programme of life can the artist and the thinker and the scientist find the preliminary foothold that enables them properly to undertake their task. To state the case in its lowest terms, only under these conditions are they able to receive an adequate, intensive training along non-utilitarian lines without hopelessly crippling their chances of self-preservation; for under these conditions they know that the social fabric is complicated enough to employ all the faculties of their minds, and that in following non-utilitarian interests they are fulfilling a recognized need of society. It is this which breeds in them the sense that they are serving something great, something so generally felt to be great that society rewards them with a pride calling forth their own pride, taking delight in setting up the sort of obstacles that constantly put them on their mettle.

Without these conditions we cannot have great leaders; without leaders we cannot have a great society. If this suggests the hope of a "national culture" to come, it is only in order that America may be able in the future to give something to the rest of the world that is better than what the world too generally means by "Americanism"—"the worship of size, mass, quantity and numbers," as a recent French essayist defines it. For three generations the most sensitive minds in Europe—Renan, Ruskin, Nietzsche, to name none more recent—have summed up their mistrust of the future in that one word; and it is because, altogether externalized ourselves, we have typified the universally externalizing influences of modern industrialism. The shame of this is a national shame, and one that the world war, with all the wealth it has brought us, has infinitely accentuated. And it covers a national problem—the problem of creating objects of loyalty within the nation by virtue of which the springs of our creative energy are touched into play.

II. THE CULTURE OF INDUSTRIALISM

I

IF WE are dreaming of a "national culture" today, it is because our inherited culture has so utterly failed to meet the exigencies of our life, to fertilize its roots. It is amazing how that fabric of ideas and assumptions, of sentiments and memories and attitudes which made up the civilization of our fathers has melted away like snow uncovering the sordid facts of a society that seems to us now so little advanced on the path of spiritual evolution. The older generation does not recognize its offspring in the crude, chaotic manifestations of the present day, but I wonder if it ever considers this universal lapse from grace in the light of cause and effect? I wonder if it ever suspects that there must have been some inherent weakness in a culture that has so lost control of a really well-disposed younger generation, a culture which, after being dominant for so long, has left in its wake a society so little civilized? What is the secret of its decay? And how does it happen that we, whose minds are gradually opening to so many living influences of the past, feel as it were the chill of the grave as we look back over the spiritual history of our last fifty years?

It was the culture of an age of pioneering, the reflex of the spirit of material enterprise—that is the obvious fact; and with the gradual decay of the impulse of enterprise, it has itself disintegrated like a mummy at the touch of sunlight. Why? Because it was never a living, active culture, releasing the creative energies of men. Its function was rather to divert these energies, to prevent the anarchical, sceptical, extravagant, dynamic forces of the spirit from taking the wind out of the myth of "progress," that myth imposed by destiny upon the imagination of our forbears in order that a great uncharted continent might be subdued to the service of the race.

For the creative impulses of men are always at war with their possessive impulses, and poetry, as we know, springs from brooding on just those aspects of experience that most retard the swift advance of the acquisitive mind. The spirit of a living culture, which ever has within it some of the acid of Pascal's phrase: "Cæsar was too old to go about conquering the world; he ought to have been more mature"—how could this ever have been permitted to grow up, even supposing that it might have been able to grow up, in a people confronted with forests and prairies and impelled by the necessities of the race to keep their hearts whole and their minds on their task? No, it was essential that everything in men should be repressed and denied that would have slackened their manual energy and made their ingenuity a thing of naught, that would have put questions into their minds, that would have made them static materially and dynamic spiritually, that would have led them to feel too much the disparity between the inherited civilization they had left behind and the environment in which they had placed themselves, that would have neutralized the spell of the exterior ambition which led them on.

Puritanism was a complete philosophy for the pioneer, and, by making human nature contemptible and putting to shame the charms of life, it unleashed the acquisitive instincts of men, disembarrassing those instincts by creating the belief that the life of the spirit is altogether a secret life and that the imagination ought never to conflict with the law of the tribe. It was this that determined the character of our old culture, which cleared the decks for practical action by draining away all the irreconcilable elements of the American nature into a transcendental upper sphere.

European critics have never been able to understand why a "young nation," living a vigorous, primitive life, should not have expressed itself artistically in a cognate form; and because Whitman did so they accepted him as the representative poet of America. So he was; but it is only now, long after the pioneer epoch has passed and the "free note" has begun to make itself heard, that he has come to seem a typical figure to his own countrypeople. In his own time, Whitman was regarded with distrust and even hatred because, by releasing, or tending to release, the creative faculties of the American mind, by exacting a poetical coöperation from his readers, he broke the pioneer law of self-preservation. By awakening people to their environment, by turning democracy from a fact into a spiritual principle, his influence ran directly counter to the necessities of the age, and his fellow-writers naturally shunned him for hitting in this way below the belt. In fact, had Whitman continued to develop along the path he originally marked out for himself, he might seriously have interfered with the logical process of the country's material evolution. But there was in Whitman himself a large share of the naïve pioneer nature, which made it impossible for him to take experience very seriously or to develop beyond a certain point. As he grew older, the sensuality of his nature led him astray in a vast satisfaction with material facts, before which he purred like a cat by the warm fire. This accounts for the reconciliation which occurred in later years between Whitman and his literary contemporaries. They saw that he had become harmless; they accepted him as a man of talent; and, making the most of his more conventional verse, they at last crowned him provisionally as the "good grey poet."

For the orthodox writers of the old school had a serious duty to perform in speeding the pioneers on their way; and they performed it with an efficiency that won them the gratitude of all their contemporaries. Longfellow, with his lullabies, crooning to sleep the insatiable creative appetites of the soul, Lowell, with his "weak-wing'd song" exalting "the deed"—how invaluable their literature was to the "tired pioneer," forerunner of the "tired business man" of the present day and only a loftier type because, like the tired soldier of the trenches, it was in response to the necessities of the race that he had dammed at their source the rejuvenating springs of the spirit. Yes, it was a great service those old writers rendered to the progress of this country's primitive development, for by unconsciously taking in charge, as it were, all the difficult elements of human nature and putting them under an anæsthesia they provided a free channel for the *élan* of their age.

But in so doing they shelved our spiritual life, conventionalizing it in a sphere above the sphere of action. In happier countries literature is the vehicle of ideals and attitudes that have sprung from experience, ideals and attitudes that release the creative impulses of the individual and stimulate a reaction in the individual against his environment. This our literature has failed to do; it has necessarily remained an exercise rather than an expression. Itself denied the principle of life or the power of giving life, it has made up for its failure to motivate the American scene and impregnate it with meaning by concentrating all its forces in the exterior field of æsthetic form. Gilding and idealizing everything it has touched, and frequently attaining a high level of imaginative style, it has thrown veils over the barrenness and emptiness of our life, putting us in extremely good conceit with ourselves while actually doing nothing either to liberate our minds or to enlighten us as to the real nature of our civilization. Hence we have the meticulous technique of our contemporary "high-class" magazines, a technique which, as we know, can be acquired as a trick, and which, artistic as it appears, is really the mark of a complete spiritual conventionality and deceives no sensible person into supposing that our general cleverness is the index of a really civilized society.

II

This virtual absence of any organic native culture has determined our response to the culture of the outer world. There are no vital relationships that are not reciprocal, and only in the measure that we undergo a cognate experience ourselves can we share in the experience of others. To the Catholic, Dante, to the aristocrat, Nietzsche, to the democrat, Whitman inevitably means more than any of them can mean to the scholar who merely receives them all through his intellect without the palpitant response of conviction and a sympathetic experience. Not that this "experience" has to be identical in the literal sense; no, the very essence of being cultivated is to have developed a capacity for sharing points of view other than our own. But there is all the difference between being actively and passively cultivated that there is between living actively or passively emotional lives. Only the creative mind can really apprehend the expressions of the creative mind. And it is because our field of action has been preëmpted by our acquisitive instincts, because in short we have no national fabric of spiritual experience, that we are so unable today to think and feel in international terms. Having ever considered it our prerogative to pluck the fruits of the spirit without undergoing the travail of generating them, having ever given to the tragi-comedy of the creative life a notional rather than a real assent, to quote Newman's famous phrase, we have been able to feed ourselves with the sugar-coating of all the bitter pills of the rest of mankind, accepting the achievements of their creative life as effects which presuppose in us no causal relationships. That is why we are so terribly at ease in the Zion of world-culture.

All this explains the ascendancy among our fathers of the Arnoldian doctrine about "knowing the best that has been thought and said in the world." For, wrapped up as they were in their material tasks, it enabled them to share vicariously in the heritage of civilization, endowing them, as it were, with all the pearls of the oyster while neatly evading in their behalf the sad responsibility of the oyster itself. It upholstered their lives with everything that is best in history, with all mankind's most sumptuous effects quite sanitarily purged of their ugly and awkward organic relationships. It set side by side in the Elysian calm of their bookshelves all the warring works of the mighty ones of the past. It made the creative life synonymous in their minds with finished things, things that repeat their message over and over and "stay put." In short, it conventionalized for them the spiritual experience of humanity, pigeon-holing it, as it were, and leaving them fancy-free to live "for practical purposes."

I remember that when, as children, we first read Carlyle and Ruskin, we were extremely puzzled by their notes of exasperated indignation. "What are they so angry about?" we wondered, and we decided that England must be a very wicked country. Presently, however, even this idea passed out of our heads, and we came to the conclusion that anger and indignation must be simply normal properties of the literary mind (as they are, in a measure) and that we ought to be grateful for this because they produce so many engaging grotesqueries of style. Our own life was so obviously ship-shape and water-tight—was it possible that people in other countries could have allowed their life to become less so? Unable as we were to decide this point, we were quite willing to give the prophets the benefit of the doubt, as regards their own people. But it was inconceivable that for us they meant any more by their emotional somersaults than the prophets of the Bible meant, whose admirably intoned objurgations we drank in with perfect composure on Sundays.

How natural, then, that the greatest, the most "difficult" European writers should have had, as Carlyle and Browning and Meredith had, their first vogue in America. How natural that we should have flocked about Ibsen, patronized Nietzsche, found something entertaining in every kind of revolutionist, and welcomed the strangest philosophies (the true quite as readily as the false). For having ourselves undergone no kindred creative experience for them to corroborate and extend, we have ever been able to escape their slings and arrows with a whole skin. They have said nothing real to us because there has been nothing in our own field of reality to make their messages real.

Consequently, those very European writers who might, under normal circumstances, have done the most to shake us out of our complacency have only served the more to confirm us in it. Our immediate sphere of action being sealed against them, their influence has been deflected into "mere literature," where it has not been actually inverted. For in so far as our spiritual appetites have been awake, it has only gone to convince us, not that we are unenlightened ourselves, but that other people are wicked. This explains the double paradox that, while our reformers never consider it necessary to take themselves in hand before they set out to improve the world, our orthodox literary men, no matter what models they place before themselves, cannot rise above the tribal view of their art as either an amusement or a soporific.

III

How then can our literature be anything but impotent? It is inevitably so, since it springs from a national mind that has been sealed against that experience from which literature derives all its values.

How true this is can be seen from almost any of its enunciations of principle, especially on the popular, that is to say the frankest, level. I open, for instance, one of our so-called better-class magazines and fall upon a character-sketch of William Gillette: "What a word! *Forget!* What a feat! What a faculty! Lucky the man who can himself forget. How gifted the one who can make others forget. It is the triumph of the art of

William Gillette that in the magic of his spell an audience forgets." Opening another magazine, I turn to a reported interview in which a well-known popular poet expatiates on his craft. "Modern life," he tells us, "is full of problems, complex and difficult, and the man who concentrates his mind on his problems all day doesn't want to concentrate it on tediously obscure poetry at night. The newspaper poets are forever preaching the sanest optimism, designed for the people who really need the influence of optimism—the bread-winners, the weary, the heavyladen. That's the kind of poetry the people want, and the fact that they want it shows that their hearts and heads are all right."

Here are two typical pronouncements of the American mind, one on the art of acting, one on the art of poetry, and they unite in expressing a perfectly coherent doctrine. This doctrine is that the function of art is to turn aside the problems of life from the current of emotional experience and create in its audience a condition of cheerfulness that is not organically derived from experience but added from the outside. It assumes that experience is not the stuff of life but something essentially meaningless; and not merely meaningless but an obstruction which retards and complicates our real business of getting on in the world and getting up in the world, and which must therefore be ignored and forgotten and evaded and beaten down by every means in our power.

What is true on the popular level is not less true on the level of serious literature, in spite of everything our most conscientious artists have been able to do. Thirty years ago, an acute English critic remarked, apropos of a novel by Howells, that our novelists seemed to regard the Civil War as an occurrence that separated lovers, not as something that ought normally to have coloured men's whole thoughts on life. And it is true that if we did not know how much our literature has to be discounted, we could hardly escape the impression, for all the documents which have come down to us, that our grandfathers really did pass through the war without undergoing the purgation of soul that is often said to justify the workings of tragic mischance in human affairs. Howells has himself given us the *comédie humaine* of our post-bellum society, Howells whose whole aim was to measure the human scope of that society, and who certainly far less than any other novelist of his time falsified his vision of reality in the interests of popular entertainment. Well, we know the sort of society Howells pictured and how he pictured it. He has himself explicitly stated, in connection with certain Russian novels, that Americans in general do not undergo the varieties of experience that Russian fiction records, that "the more smiling aspects of life" are "the more American," and that in being true to our "well-to-do actualities" the American novelist does all that can be expected of him. Could one ask for a more essential declaration of artistic bankruptcy than that?

For what does it amount to, this declaration? It identifies the reality of the artist's vision with what is accepted as reality in the world about him. But every one knows that the sketchiest, the most immature, the most trivial society is just as susceptible as any other of the most profound artistic reconstruction; all that is required is an artist capable of penetrating beneath it. The great artist floats the visible world on the sea of his imagination, and measures it, not by its own scale of values, but by the scale of values he has himself derived from his descent into the abysses of life. What, then, is amiss with our writers? They are victims of the universal taboo which the ideal of material success, of the acquisitive life, has placed upon experience. It matters not at all that they have no part or lot in this ideal, that they are men of the finest artistic conscience. In the first place, from their earliest childhood they are taught to repress everything that conflicts with the material welfare of their environment; in the second place, their environment is itself so denatured, so stripped of everything that might nourish the imagination, that they do not so much mature at all as externalize themselves in a world of externalities. Unable to achieve a sufficiently active consciousness of themselves to return upon their environment and overthrow it and dissolve it and recreate it in the terms of a personal vision, they gradually come to accept it on its own terms. If Boston is their theme, they become Bostonian; if it is the Yukon, they become "abysmal brutes"; if it is nature, nature becomes the hero of their work; and if it is machinery, the machines themselves become vocal and express their natural contempt for a humanity that is incapable, either morally or artistically, of putting them in their place and keeping them there.

We know how this occurred with Howells. "It seemed to me then, and for a good while afterward," he writes in *Literary Friends and Acquaintances*, apropos of his first reception by the Boston Olympians of the sixties, "that a person who had seen the men and had the things said before him that I had in Boston, could not keep himself too carefully in cotton; and this was what I did all the following winter, though of course it was a secret between me and me." Never, assuredly, in any other society, has literary hero-worship taken quite the complexion of that; for the statement is accurately true. Such was the prestige of Boston and the pundits of Boston that Howells, having cast his anchor in its lee, scarcely felt, at least for a long while, the necessity of exploring, on his own account, beyond the spacious, quiet harbour of life that presented itself to the cultivated New England eye. The result may be seen in such novels as *A Modern Instance*, the tragedy of which is viewed not from the angle of an experience that is wider and deeper, as the experience of a great novelist always is, than that of any character the novelist's imagination is able to conceive, but from the angle of Ben Halleck, the epitome of Boston's best public opinion. Boston passes judgment, and Howells concurs; and one closes the book feeling that one has seen life through the eye not of a free personality but of a highly conventional community at a given epoch.*

It is exactly the same, to ignore a thousand incidental distinctions, in the work of Jack London. Between the superman of European fiction and Jack London's superman there is all the difference that separates an ideal achieved in the mind of the writer and a fact accepted from the world outside him; all the difference, in short, that separates the truth of art from the appearance of life. If these, therefore, among the freshest and most original talents our fiction has known since Hawthorne's day, have been absorbed in an atmosphere which no one has ever been able to condense, is it remarkable that the rank and file have slipped and fallen, that they have never learned to stand upright and possess themselves? Is it remarkable that they sell themselves out at the first bid, that they dress out their souls in the ready-made clothes the world offers them?

* Howells's well-known remark, "Few are worthy to live in Boston" (1866), was uttered without irony. But later, one must heartily admit, his view of life was much more universal.

Such, in fact, is the deficiency of personal impulse, of the creative will, in America, so overwhelming is the demand laid upon Americans to serve ulterior and impersonal ends, that it is as if their springs of spiritual action had altogether evaporated. Launched in a society where individuals and their faculties appear only to pass away, almost wholly apart from and without acting upon one another, our writers find themselves enveloped in an impalpable atmosphere that acts as a perpetual dissolvent of the whole field of reality both within and without themselves, an atmosphere that invades every province of life and takes its discount from everything they can do, an atmosphere that prevents the formation of oases of reality in the universal chaos. Is it remarkable that they take refuge in the abstract, the non-human, the impersonal, in the "bigness" of the phenomenal world, in the surface values of "local colour," and in the "social conscience," which enables them to do so much good by writing badly that they often come to think of artistic truth itself as an enemy of progress?

IV

Thus, because it possesses none of those values which endow life with a significance in and of itself, values which art and literature alone can give, the American mind has been gradually subdued to what it has worked in. It has had no barriers to throw up against the overwhelming material forces that have beleaguered it. Consequently, it has gone out of itself as it were and assumed the values of its environment.

Of this the most obvious example is the peculiar optimism, the so-called systematic optimism, that can be fairly taken as what psychologists call the "total reaction upon life" of the typical American mind of the last twenty years.* Mr. Horace Fletcher has defined this optimism in terms that leave no doubt of its being at once an effect and a cause of our spiritual impotence:

Optimism can be prescribed and applied as a medicine. Is there anything new and practical in this or is it but a continuation of the endless discussion of the philosophy of life, morals, medicine, etc.? Is it something that a busy person may put into practice, take with him to his business, without interfering with his business, and profit by; and, finally, what does it cost? Does adoption of it involve discharging one's doctor-friend, displeasing one's pastor, alienating one's social companions, or shocking the sacred traditions that were dear to father and mother? It is ameliorative, preventive, and harmonizing; and also it is easy, agreeable, ever available, and altogether profitable. By these hall-marks of Truth we know that it is true.

Grotesque as this may seem, you will search in vain for a more accurate presentation of the workaday point of view of our tumbling American world. This is the way most Americans think, and what they think, whether they profess the religion of mind-cure, uplift, sunshine, popular pragmatism, the gospel of advertising, or plain business; and they mean exactly what the beauty-experts mean when they say, "Avoid strong emotions if you wish to retain a youthful complexion." Systematic optimism, in other words, effects a complete revaluation of values and enthrones truth upon a conception of animal success the prerequisite of which is a thorough-going denial and evasion of emotional experience. It is the chronic result of contact with a prodigal nature too easily borne under by a too great excess of will, of opportunities so abundant and so al-

* Written in 1916.

luring that we have been led to suppress the creative spirit in ourselves, traditionally unaware as we are of the mature potentialities and justifications of human nature, and establish our scale of values in the incomparably rich material territory that surrounds us. If today, therefore, we find no principle of integrity at work in any department of our life, if religion competes with advertising, art competes with trade, and trade gives itself out as philanthropy, if we present to the world at large the spectacle of a vast undifferentiated herd of good-humoured animals, it is because we have passively surrendered our human values at the demand of circumstance.

III. YOUNG AMERICA

> "When first hatched they are free-swimming microscopic creatures, but in a few hours they fall to the bottom and are lost unless they can adhere to a firm, clean surface while making their shells and undergoing development."
>
> *Report on the Oyster Industry*

WHEN I speak of the culture of industrialism, I do not mean to imply that it has been peculiar to us. Everywhere the industrial process has devitalized men and produced a poor quality of human nature. By virtue of this process, the culture of the whole Western world fell too largely, during the nineteenth century, into the hands of the prig and the æsthete, those two sick blossoms of the same sapless stalk, whose roots have been for so long unwatered by the convictions of the race. But in Europe the great traditional culture, the culture that has ever held up the flame of the human spirit, has never been quite gutted out. The industrialism that bowled us over, because for generations our powers of resistance had been undermined by Puritanism, was no sooner well under way in Europe than human nature began to get its back up, so to speak; and a long line of great rebels reacted violently against its desiccating influences. Philologists like Nietzsche and Renan, digging among the roots of Greek and Semitic thought, artists like Morris and Rodin, rediscovering the beautiful and happy art of the Middle Ages, economists like Marx and Mill, revolting against the facts of their environment, kept alive the tradition of a great society, and great ways of living, and thus were able to assimilate for human uses the positive by-products of industrialism itself, science and democracy. They made it impossible for men to forget the degradation of society and the poverty of their lives and built a bridge between the greatness of the few in the past and the greatness of the many, perhaps, in the future. Thus the democracies of Europe are richer than ours in self-knowledge, possessing ideals grounded in their own field of reality and so providing them with a constant stimulus to rise above their dead selves, never doubting that experience itself is worth having lived for, even if it leads to nothing else. And thus, however slowly they advance, they advance on firm ground.

For us, individually and socially, as I have tried to show, nothing of this kind has been possible. It seems to me symbolic of our society that the only son of Abraham Lincoln should have become the president of the Pullman Company, that the son of the man who liberated the slaves politically should have been the first, as *The Nation* pointed out not long ago, to exploit them industrially. Our disbelief in experience, our habitual repression of the creative instinct, our consequent over-stimulation of the acquisitive instinct, has made it impossible for us to take advantage of the treasures our own life has yielded. Democracy and science, for example, have *happened to us* abundantly, more abundantly perhaps than to others because they have had less inertia to overcome; but, like children presented with shining gold-pieces, we have not known how to use them. Either we have been unable to distinguish them from copper pennies, or else we have spent them in foolish ways that have made us ill. Our personal life has in no way contributed to the enriching of our environment; our environment, in turn, has given us personally no sense of the significance of life.

We of the younger generation, therefore, find ourselves in a grave predicament. For having, unlike Europeans of any class, no fund of spiritual experience in our blood, as it were, to balance the various parts of our natures, we are all but incapable of coördinating ourselves in a free world. We are no longer able to make the sort of "go" of life our fathers made: the whole spirit of our age is against the dualism which they accepted as a matter of course. The acquisitive life has lost the sanction of necessity which the age of pioneering gave it. A new age has begun, an age of intensive cultivation, and it is the creative life that the nation calls for now. But for that how ill-equipped we are! Our literature has prepared no pathways for us, our leaders are themselves lost. We are like explorers who, in the morning of their lives, have deserted the hearthstone of the human tradition and have set out for a distant treasure that has turned to dust in their hands; but, having on their way neglected to mark their track, they no longer know in which direction their home lies, nor how to reach it, and so they wander in the wilderness, consumed with a double consciousness of waste and impotence.

I think this fairly describes the frame of mind of a vast number of Americans of the younger generation. They find themselves born into a race that has drained away all its spiritual resources in the struggle to survive and that continues to struggle in the midst of plenty because life itself no longer possesses any other meaning. The gradual commercialization of all the professions, meanwhile, has all but entirely destroyed the possibility of personal growth along the lines that our society provides and, having provided, sanctions. Brought up as they have been to associate activity almost solely with material ends, and unable in this overwhelmingly prosperous age to feel any powerful incentive to seek these ends, acutely conscious of their spiritual unemployment and impoverished in will and impulse, the more sensitive minds of the younger generation drift almost inevitably into a state of internal anarchism that finds outlet, where it finds outlet at all, in a hundred unproductive forms.

Our society, in fact, which does everything by wholesale, is rapidly breeding a race of Hamlets the like of which has hardly been seen before, except perhaps in nineteenth-century Russia. Nothing is more remarkable than the similarity in this respect between the two immense inchoate populations that flank Europe on east and west. To be sure, the Oblomovs and Bazarovs and Levins and Dmitri Rudins of Russian fiction are in many ways, like Hamlet himself, universal characters. But for one Hamlet in an organized society which, according to the measure of its organization, provides an outlet for every talent, there are twenty in a society which, as we say, has no use for its highly developed types. And that is the situation both in Russia and in the United States: the social fabric is too simple to be able to cope with the complicated strain that has been suddenly put upon it by a radical change in the conditions of life. Yet in each case the complexities have developed along just the lines most necessary for the rounded well-being of society. The Hamlets of Russian fiction, generally speaking, are social idealists, wrapped up in dreams of agricultural and educational reform; they long to revolutionize their country estates and ameliorate the lot of their peasantry, and they lose their will and their vision because there is no social machinery of which they can avail themselves: thrown as they are upon their own unaided resources, their task overwhelms them at the outset with a sense of futility. Turn the tables about, and we have the situation of the corresponding class in America. They find the machinery of education and social welfare in a state as highly developed as the life of the spirit is in Russia; it is the spiritual technique that is wanting, a living culture, a complicated scheme of ideal objectives, upheld by society at large, enabling them to submerge their liberties in their loyalties and to unite in the task of building up a civilization.

In short, owing to the miraculous rapidity and efficiency with which we have been able to effect the material conquest of the continent, a prodigious amount of energy has been thrown out of employment which our society is unable to receive and set to work. All the innate spirituality of the American nature, dammed up, stagnant from disuse, has begun to pour itself out in a vast flood of undisciplined emotionalism that goes—how often!—to waste. It goes to waste largely because the scope of our "useful" objectives is so restricted, and because, inheriting as we do an ingrained individualism, an ingrained belief in quick returns, we are all but unable to retain these treacherous elements, of which we have had so little practical experience in the past, until they have reached a sufficient maturity to take shape in lasting forms.

But this new individualism, which finds its gospel in

self-expression, is totally different from the individualism of the past. The old spiritual individualism was blood-brother to the old materialistic individualism: it throve in the same soil and produced a cognate type of mind. It was hard, stiff-necked, combative, opinionative, sectarian, self-willed; it gave birth, along with several men of genius, to the crank, the shrill, high-strung propounder of strange religions, the self-important monopolist of truth. In short, it was essentially competitive. The new individualism, on the other hand, is individualistic only by default; its individualistic character, so to say, is only an inherited bad habit, a bad habit that is perpetuated by the want of objectives in the truly vacuous world with which it finds itself confronted. It has, I think, no desire to vaunt itself; it tends, instead of this, to lavish itself; it is not combative, it is coöperative, not opinionative but groping, not sectarian but filled with an intense, confused eagerness to identify itself with the life of the whole people. If it remains confused, if it is unable to discipline itself, if it is often lazy and wilful, if its smoke is only at intervals illuminated by flame—well, was it not just so with the Oblomovs of Russia? Who could *wish* to be confused and lazy, especially if he has no material motives to console him in other ways? Men who do not "burn with a hard, gem-like flame" are simply men who cannot feel that they are employed by civilization.

Undoubtedly the gospel of self-expression, makeshift as it is, has revealed a promise in America that we have always taken for granted but hardly reckoned with. Isolated, secretive, bottled up as we have been in the past, how could we ever have guessed what aims and hopes we have in common had they not been brought to light, even in the crudest and most inadequate ways? That they have at last been brought to light I think few will deny; but will they advance further? Only, it seems to me, if we are able to build up, to adapt a phrase from the slang of politics, a programme for the conservation of our spiritual resources.

"Humanity," wrote Mazzini in 1858, "is a great army marching to the conquest of unknown lands, against enemies both strong and cunning. The peoples are its corps, each with its special operation to carry out, and the common victory depends on the exactness with which they execute the different operations." That nationalities are the workshops of humanity, that each nationality has a special duty to perform, a special genius to exert, a special gift to contribute to the general stock of civilization, and that each, in consequence, growing by the trust that other nationalities place in it, must be a living, homogeneous entity, with its own faith and consciousness of self—could any idea more perfectly than this express the dream, the necessity, of Young America? To live creatively, to live completely, to live in behalf of some great corporate purpose—that is its desire. A national faith we had once, a national dream, the dream of the "great American experiment." But if it had not been sadly compromised, would the younger generation find itself adrift as it is today? Too many elements of that old faith of ours were at war with all that was good in it, and it admitted too few of the factors of life; it was betrayed by what was false within; it was unable to embrace the freer impulses of a new time. That is why it contributes so little to the new faith without which America cannot live.

To discover that faith, to formulate that new technique, to build up, as I have said, that programme for the conservation of our spiritual resources, is the task of criticism and philosophy. Our critics and philosophers, I think, have thus far shirked this task. Why, and in what degree, I hope to suggest in the following chapters.

IV. OUR CRITICS

IN A famous essay, Matthew Arnold said that it is "the business of the critical power to see the object as in itself it really is." If any of our critics had been able to act upon this principle, if they had been able to put aside their prepossessions and merely open their minds to the facts of American life, even without attempting any of the more heroic measures our life notoriously demands, I think the predicament of the younger generation would be far less grave than it is. For, as Arnold goes on to say, by seeing the object as in itself it really is, criticism "tends to make an intellectual situation of which the creative power can profitably avail itself." There, surely, is the very thing that Young America needs. Deficient as it is in creative power, it has more creative desire than it knows what to do with; and is it not a situation of which it can profitably avail itself that turns desire into power? If our critics have failed to make that situation, they can hardly hold Young America responsible for the chaos that now debilitates it. The responsibility, I think, lies rather upon our critics themselves.

For the truth is that, far from "seeing the object as in itself it really is," our critics do not see the object, for them the supreme object, America, the living creative life of America, at all. That is only natural perhaps in the pundits of our criticism, Paul Elmer More and Irving Babbitt, for example, who feel that there is little worth seeing in a world Rousseau has perverted. And perhaps it is not surprising in such sensitive minds of the older generation as Mr. Brownell and Mr. Woodberry, who responded so passionately in their youth to visions of grace that never could have been ours, that they have no heart for the homelier tasks of America. But, remarkably, it is just as true of those more complacent and sometimes all too complacent critics of the middle generation who feel themselves in life apparently by no means alien to the stirring American scene. Interest, mere friendly interest, for severe interest we cannot expect, is the last boon our critics yield us. Is it strange, then, that our creative life halts and stammers in bewilderment?

It is certainly remarkable, this apparently general determination not to be practical on the part of so many dissimilar minds; and it is all the more remarkable because criticism has ever been, in other countries, precisely the most practical of the literary arts. Since the days when Socrates, its august founder, sat in the market-place and played the midwife to so many inarticulate minds, it has been the joyous prerogative of criticism to be on the spot when thoughts are being born. Not to mention any names that the most academic of our critics can gainsay, is it not the glory of Lessing that he established a sort of norm of the German character, descending into the thick of reality and building, by creation and controversy alike, amid the shifting sands of pedantry and exoticism, an impregnable base for the superstructure of a civilization to come? As for Sainte-Beuve, he lived in an age and a society that required no such drastic restatements of fundamental truth; he inherited and perpetuated that marvellous equilibrium of the French temper which is the result of an organic culture founded on the suffrages of the whole race. But Sainte-Beuve lived and wrote in substantial harmony with the creative life of his contemporaries, and he, too, was ever ready to spring to the defence of new-born thoughts and fight for their just rights of passage into the French mind. No doubt in the France of Sainte-Beuve there were more new-born thoughts worth fighting for, strictly as thoughts, than there are in the America of today. But no one denies that at present in this country an immense amount of creative energy has at least conclusively turned itself towards the field of the arts. If it does not in many instances come rightly and fully to a head, if it fails very often to eventuate in thoughts in themselves vitally important, does it not all the more behoove criticism to condense the vapours that confuse this creative energy and to spring loyally to the support of groping minds that bear the mark of sincerity and promise? As for our critics, what birth out of life have any of them ever defended with that heavy artillery they so enjoy training upon those popular American fallacies many of which, quite plainly, are the result of their own immemorial absentee-mindedness? Have they ever been at pains to grasp the contemporary American mind and its problems, to discover what the contemporary American mind is, and what it is capable of, and how it can best be approached, and whether it is able to assimilate the culture of the world before it has formed any personal conception of what culture is?

Our critics, if they are in touch with European life,

must be aware that the relation in which they stand to the life of their own country is quite unique. But far even from considering the idea that the living forces about them deserve a little sympathetic and discreet attention, they seem to be persuaded that the younger generation presents a united front against everything that mankind has tried and found worthy, and that it has formed a sort of conspiracy to propagate falsehood at whatever cost. "What Matthew Arnold would call 'the elephantine main body,' " says Mr. Babbitt, "seems more convinced than ever that man, to become perfect, has only to continue indefinitely the programme of the nineteenth century—that is, to engage in miscellaneous expansion and back it up if need be with noisy revolt against all the forms of the past." To which Mr. Brownell subjoins the following: "Every one who sympathetically 'belongs' to [the age] feels himself stanchly supported by the consensus of all it esteems. . . . The militancy of the age therefore finds itself not only in possession of a perfectly definite—if mainly destructive—credo, but of a practically united and enthusiastic army."

To us who are so much in the thick of things that we cannot see the forest for the trees, statements of this kind are all but unintelligible. They seem to us like anathemas delivered in some half-forgotten sacred language to a people that has begun to stammer in a vernacular of its own. We are so conscious of our own differences, of the hundred and one programmes that we are pursuing precisely *not* in common, that while we are prepared for body-blows from Mr. Babbitt (to whose vigorous intellect, by the way, many of us are greatly indebted), we scarcely know what to make of Mr. Brownell's more graciously delivered thrusts. But we may be very sure that if, to the older generation, we appear to be a "practically united and enthusiastic army," we must be so in some sense in which the older generation is not. To what that sense *is*, our critics themselves, in a general way, have given us the clue. They say that we are emotional, and they give to their accusation an air of plausibility by adding that we are over-emotional, as, in fact, we are; but what they really object to is that we are emotional at all, the strength of their own case resting wholly on the assumption that literature ought to spring not from the emotions but from the intellect. This we deny, and I suppose that our denial is so unanimous that it does, in a way, neutralize our intellectual differences. But why do we deny it? Partly because our reaction upon life, on the one hand, and our reading of the history of literature, on the other, leads us to believe that it is false; and partly because we have witnessed the failure and breakdown of intellectualism itself.

Consider, for example, Mr. More, our chief exponent of the intellectualist position. Mr. More, referring to the "yellow press," delivers himself of the following remarks: "On days when no sensational event has occurred, it will indulge in the prettiest sentimental sermons on the home and on family felicities. . . . But let the popular mind be excited by some crime of lust, and the same journal will forget the sweet obligations of home and wife . . . and will deck out the loathsome debauchery of a murderer and his trull as the spiritual history of two young souls finding themselves in the pure air of passion." Now, really, whatever the provocations of the yellow press, can one imagine a piece of worse literary breeding than this? Yet it can almost be called Mr. More's habitual tone whenever, leaving the charmed circle of literary ideas, he deals with modern society. Far from being reasonable and humane, his note is one of nagging, pettish, and one would almost say vulgar exasperation; he betrays a tendency to break out on every occasion into promiscuous abuse. How then can our intellectualists expect to convert us to the music of the classical discipline when some of their own most representative minds—for Mr. More is by no means unique as an advocate of "the classic point of view"—are so singularly ill-nurtured? If this is what the classical discipline does—how can we avoid being led, quite unjustly, to conclude?—let us by all means turn to the discipline of science which produced the ever just and ever genial William James.

That is what we mean when we speak of the breakdown of intellectualism; for of course the reason why Mr. More's humane attitude cracks and crumbles so at the touch of life is because it is based on a culture of the intellect that is not borne out by a corresponding culture of the feelings. Mr. More's emotional life, as his writings exhibit it, is just as crude and untempered as the intellectual life of the younger generation which he attacks. Why is this so? Because Mr. More's intellectualism is the converse and counterpart of the materialism that has led to the younger generation's incapacity to accept the discipline he offers it. He has not been able to feel human values finely because to have done so would have been to upset his faith in a society based not upon the creative instincts but upon the acquisitive instincts of men, a society ruled by the "natural aristocracy" of economic power. Mr. More is a belated pioneer, with all the repressed impulses, the fundamental limitations, the exaggerated antipathies that belong to the pioneer type, extended and subtilized in the sphere of the intellect alone. Turn from his philosophical and literary essays, in which he is able to be humane at large, to his essays on social and economic themes, and see how quickly he lets the cat out of the bag. "Looking at the larger good of society," he observes, "we may say that the dollar is more than the man and that *the rights of property are more important than the right to life.*"

Here, then, we have a clue not merely to the breakdown of the intellectualist point of view but to its origin as well. Mr. Brownell says that we used to have in this country a public comparable with those *honnêtes gens*, equally removed from a court that was too rigid and a pit that was too free, through which the French tradition was so long maintained. "A public like this," he says, "we once had, and we have it no longer. Its limitations were marked, but they emphasized its existence. Its standards were narrow, but it had standards. We had a class, not numerous but fairly defined, corresponding to the class Charles Sumner found in England, distinct from the nobility but possessed in abundance of serious knowledge, high accomplishment, and refined taste, the class, precisely, called by Molière *les honnêtes gens*." Now, that such a class did exist at one time in this country no one who has any associations with our past could possibly deny. But that this class actually corresponded with the *honnêtes gens* of France one might perhaps be permitted to question, even if André Gide, to whom Mr. Brownell refers, had not remarked that in France itself the tradition they maintained would hardly have been possible without the court. But why did the existence of the court make so much difference? Because the court, removed as it was from the influences of the market-place, kept alive in France the free, the non-acquisitive, in short the creative conception of life; and this conception, permeating thence downward the whole fabric of society, linked the artistic expressions at the top with the common consciousness of the race beneath, a common consciousness that has never denied its Rabelaisian elements. Between these two extremes, then, of racial experience and racial expression, and partaking abundantly of both, the *honnêtes gens*, with their "serious knowledge, their high accomplishment, their refined taste" formed a sort of mean, logically poised. French wit, French elegance, French taste—are they not, as Mr. Brownell himself would be the first to point out, simply the polished outside, the polished extremity, as it were, of a social mass that is modelled and civilized all the way through, according to its own genius, a social mass all the strata of which are fused and unified, and which is grounded imperturbably on the basis of a common experience of life? It is quite true, as Mr. Brownell says, that Molière would never have written his best work had he practised only on his cook. But is there not a certain difference between French society and our own in the fact that Molière was able to practise on his cook at all?

For our cultivated class of old never demanded, never assumed the existence of, and never attempted to create—how could it have done so?—a common ground of experience in the American people. It accepted men as "infinitely repellent particles" and drew them together by projecting a spirit that appealed to their intellect and their will alone and that never conflicted with the full exercise of their instincts of acquisition. Having neither, on the one hand, "a court that was too rigid" but that would, nevertheless, have preserved the creative conception of life, nor, on the other, "a pit that was too free" but that would, equally, have kept them in touch with a level of primitive emotional life, our cultivated class, with their serious knowledge, their high accomplishment, their refined taste, were suspended in the air, so to speak, deprived alike of the creative spark that lifts men above themselves and the animal under-proppings that maintain their contact with rude reality. Our old writers established as a common ground between themselves and their readers either the non-human world of external nature (Thoreau), the world of the will (Emerson), the world of memory and association (Longfellow), the emotion of special causes like abolition or the Civil War (Whittier, Lowell) or of special occasions (Holmes), but seldom, if ever, the congruous world of human life in general. They knew that their neighbours and that extended neighbourship which constituted their public had no emotional life in common because their existence on the active plane was a competitive one; bent as their public was on "getting on" individually, how could they admit or cultivate an inner community as social beings? Admit it of course they could not, neither could they cultivate it; and the result was that our old culture never was and never became organic: a by-product of the conditions of its time, it was unable to project itself beyond those conditions. That is why it strikes one as so futile when Mr. Brownell pleads for the extension of taste without taking into consideration the primitive forces that will have to undergo a profound transmutation before taste in the organic sense will really be possible in America. *Inorganic* taste we already have in abundance, and every year, following the spread of wealth, it increases more and more. Nowadays a little money and a little training and a little expert advice enable almost anyone to possess a "flawless" drawing room, for example (especially if he keeps within the safe circle of the neutral colours). But is it not abundantly evident that this very general attainment of æsthetic taste is quite compatible with an extreme want of taste in other relations of life?

Upon almost all our social relations, in fact, the effect is so obvious of our competitive, non-creative past that, were it not that our critics belong to that competitive, non-creative past and cannot escape from its circle of ideas, it would seem almost wanton of them to accuse the younger generation of having created a chaos which, in truth, they have only become conscious of. Our critics themselves have always said that our society is too incongruous to produce a high social comedy; but why do they draw the line there? Do they not see that "high" literature in any *genre*, literature, I mean, that is based on a complicated social understanding, is all but impossible for us at present, except on a forced and artificial plane? Consider Dr. Crothers, for example. Why are the essays of Dr. Crothers so self-conscious if it is not because Dr. Crothers knows perfectly well that his eighty thousand readers have no emotional life in common either with him or with each other, because he does not feel *at home* with his readers as Charles Lamb felt, or even as Dr. Holmes felt in his little Harvard world of the past? They admit, I suppose, that Dr. Crothers is self-conscious; but why do they accept his self-consciousness with only a gesture of deprecation while they attack in so savage a way the self-consciousness of the younger generation? Because, while the self-consciousness of the younger generation stands for an instinctive drive towards a common understanding on the creative plane, the self-consciousness of Dr. Crothers, making no levy upon our creative life, accepts the pioneer law of self-preservation, in the scheme of which literature is only a kind of associational and secondary play of the mind in a society whose real business is the art of getting on.

Our critics are thus unable to connect with the creative life of the present because they are precluded from so doing by the programme of the epoch in which they were bred. Mr. Babbitt and Mr. Brownell differ from Mr. More in being instinctively humane minds; but they are sympathetic, none the less, with Mr. More's pioneer sociology; they have simply not filled out their points of view on the economic and psychological sides, and thus, without deliberately repudiating, they ignore the economic and psychological interpretations of life according to which literature is not an entity in itself but one of the manifestations of society. Here is a statement in point from Mr. Babbitt's *New Laokoön:* "Lessing repudiated what was artificial and superficial in the French tradition—its conventions, and etiquette, and gallantries—but at the risk of losing a real virtue, viz., the exquisite urbanity that the French at their best had really succeeded in attaining." Mr. Babbitt, as we see, implies that literature and society are distinct entities following separate laws. For only on the assumption that literature is independent of society and not, as Madame de Staël said a hundred years ago, an expression of it, only on the assumption, that is to say, that literature forms a self-sufficient world, is it possible to dream that you can pick out all the plums from the literary pudding and make a nice little particular pie for yourself. How could this "exquisite urbanity" of the French tradition have been anything but exotic in the Berlin of 1760? And how could it possibly have been preserved when those other characteristics of the French tradition, with which it was organically bound up, had been repudiated? Was it not, in fact, the great work of Lessing, that work, not so much of intelligence as of character, for which, according to Goethe, the Germans have so revered his memory, that he purged the German mind of *all* its exotic elements and grounded its literature in the firm subsoil of its own nature? Our critics, to repeat, maintain this peculiar eclecticism partly because, not being creative minds, they do not appreciate, as the creative mind does, the necessary correspondence between expression and experience, even, if need be, the most limited and local experience, and partly because by means of it they are able to prevent literature from coming into direct contact with a society whose acquisitive, non-creative programme it would immediately upset and destroy.

Naturally, therefore, they find in the recent tendencies of our literature nothing but sound and fury, signifying nothing. Nor can they themselves suggest any principles of order adapted to a spiritually unorganized society.

V. OUR AWAKENERS

I

In that very interesting testament, *Literature in Ireland*, which he left for his fellow-poets, Thomas MacDonagh showed how disadvantageous it is to have a full-grown criticism side by side with what he calls a baby literature. "There is," he says, "a school of criticism in Ireland, a school that knows the work of the finest critics in the world, and knows too, what is more important, the finest literature in the world. This, when dealing with literature in general, adds to the store of fine critical work. This at times encourages and approves good original Irish work. I think it unfortunate, however, that it should have grown with, or indeed before, the original work. Dealing with the monuments of the older literatures—English, French, and the like—this criticism knows its place, its bearings, its conditions. Dealing with a naissant literature it looks over its shoulder, as it were. Its neck is awry. Its eyes are twisted round. Its feet turn from their known way and stumble. When it does get a clear view of its object, it misses the shapes and forms it saw in other lands and expresses its disappointment."

Of our own criticism, surely, of our own critics, one could hardly have a better description than that. For Ireland and America really are alike in that they inherit a dominant academic tradition, colonial in essence, having its home in centres of civilization remote from the springs of a national life which has only of late come into its own consciousness. For the shaping of that consciousness, therefore, we cannot look to our critics for any assistance. Far from being guides and friends of the creative spirit about them, they have rather been driven to destroy in others the poet that has died in themselves.

But, after all, our critics have never set up to be national awakeners. They have never pretended to be on terms of intimacy with the real conditions of our life; they know in their own hearts, I think, that they cannot suggest any way out of our difficulties. Who, then, are, or who purport to be, our real awakeners? The sociologists whose doctrine is the adaptation of man to his environment, the apostles of a narrow efficiency, and the pragmatic and realistic philosophers who stand behind them. For twenty years and more now they have occupied the centre of our life. They have not only accepted reality, they have claimed reality, they have said that they alone apprehend reality, and that reality has been put in their special charge because they alone are able to do something with it. Well, and here we are. They have asked us to judge them by their fruits. What are we to say?

For the influence of these awakeners of ours has been, directly or indirectly, universal; their philosophy has been the formulation, the rationalization of the whole spirit of our life at least since the Spanish-American war. And observe the condition in which we now are: sultry, flaccid, hesitant, not knowing what we want and incapable of wanting anything very much, certainly not in love with our life, certainly not at home in this field of reality our awakeners have bidden us to be at home in, inclined as ever to substitute monetary for real values, and to stand in mortal fear of letting loose the spiritual appetites that impede our pursuit of a neat, hygienic and sterile success. What, in fact, *is* the note of our society today? A universal tepidity, it seems to me, the faded offspring of the Puritan hatred of human nature, which makes perhaps a majority of our kindly fellow-countrymen seem quite incapable of living, loving, thinking, dreaming or hoping with any degree of passion or intensity, pacifistic at bottom not from any specific realization of war but from a distaste for the militant life *in toto*. We know this only too well; it is the secret of our humiliation, and it explains the desire of so many people to see this country jolted and shaken up. What can our awakeners say to all this? It is not their fault, certainly, that things are so; but so things are, and it is in the days of their consulate that things have become so. Out of pragmatism our new leadership has been recruited—the leadership of "interpretation." If at last that leadership has revealed itself as no leadership at all, I think it is because pragmatism, by default, has got itself into a false position.

By default, I say; for not content with remaining a method, it has, owing to the impotence of our poetical tradition, attempted to fill the place which poetry alone can adequately fill, and which our poetry, in its complacent animalism, on the one hand, and its complicated escape from reality on the other, has left vacant. That is to say, it has assumed the right to formulate the aims of life and the values by which those aims are tested, aims and values which, we are led by history to believe, can be effectively formulated only by individual minds not in harmony with the existing fact but in revolt against it. Social efficiency is the ideal posited by John Dewey. But an ideal is an end, and social efficiency is not an end; it is a means towards the realization of human values. Has not the purpose, has not even the *scope* of social efficiency always been determined by individuals who from time to time repudiate the social organism altogether and, rising themselves to a fresh level, drag mankind after them? Life proceeds not by the burnishing up of existent ideals, but by the discovery of new and more vital ideals, thanks to the imagination, which reaches out into an unknown whither the intelligence is able to follow only after a long interval. Does not pragmatism therefore turn the natural order of things inside out when it accepts the intelligence instead of the imagination as the value-creating entity? It does, virtually if not absolutely, and in so doing crowds out and replaces the essential factor from which all dynamic creativity springs. It becomes, in a word, the dog in the manger of our creative life. What if it is an amiable, friendly dog with none of the other disagreeable proclivities of the dog in the fable? The main thing is that it occupies the crib that belongs to the winged horse of poetry. That is why we have no right to object when the winged horse suddenly opens his mouth and remarks in the words of Æsop: "What a miserable cur! He cannot eat corn himself, nor will he allow others to eat it who can."

Had not the pragmatists issued a special claim upon reality, had they not, a little arrogantly, assumed the rights of leadership, no one would hold them responsible now for the general aimlessness of our life. Drift is their abhorrence too, and in many directions they have pointed out the road to mastery. Moreover, pragmatism was formulated by two thinkers who, in their feeling for reality, in their acceptance of a human nature that calls nothing common or unclean, and in their desire to make human nature more conscious of itself, might well be called rather poets than philosophers. They were poets, yes; but they were not sufficiently poets to intensify the conception of human nature they had inherited from our tradition. Their own vein of poetry, golden in William James, silver in John Dewey, ran too thin for that; and besides, their whole training had gone to make them students of the existing fact. Unable as they were to alter the level of human vision, all they could do was to take men on the level where they found them and release their latent capacities on that level—an immensely valuable thing, of course, but not the vital thing for us, because it is the level itself that is at fault in America. Had our existing fact, had the core of our life been sufficiently rich, then their programme of liberation and control would have been as adequate for the nation in general as it now is for the few qualified individuals. What it actually did was to unfold, for the most part, a human nature that was either detached from the sources of life or contented with a very primitive range of needs and desires.

That is why, though they are always cutting off the heads of the hydra that has us in its grasp, our pragmatic awakeners have really not only failed us but traduced us. For our hydra is, and always has been, self-complacency, satisfaction with just the primitive scale of human values I speak of; and self-complacency, as a spiritual fact, is proof against all the arrows of the intelligence. Our awakeners accept themselves as a norm and by so doing become themselves a part of the very hydra that they attack. Assuming that the intelligence is the final court of appeal, they are sealed against those impulses that give birth to self-criticism and the principle of growth; all they can do, therefore, is to unfold the existing fact in themselves, and in the world about them.

Does it matter that the founders of pragmatism, like certain of its English congeners, H. G. Wells, for example, have passed outside it in order to meet the critical issues of life? The mercurial pilgrim soul of William James had passed on to a strange polytheistic mysticism long before he died; H. G. Wells, under the stress of the war, redoubled his quest of "God, the Invisible King"; and John Dewey has not denied the need of a national faith in this country, to attain which we shall certainly have not merely to do something other than we normally do, but to be something other than we normally are. Creators themselves, and essentially poets, they have been free of their own creations, they have shown that they are members of the elect company of the "older and bolder"; nevertheless, they have justified a multitude of their followers in that complacent, mechanistic view of life to which everything else in our mock-efficient, success-loving society predisposes them. Enthroning, as they have, the intelligence which merely sees, in place of the imagination which sees and feels, they have, in their "practicality," sanctioned the type of mind whose emotional needs are so limited that the efficient pursuit of some special object is all that it demands of life.

II

Pragmatism has failed us, I say, because it has attempted to fill the place that only a national poetry can adequately fill. Does any one imagine that we are the only people that has been reduced to the pulp-like, inelastic state in which we find ourselves today? Have we forgotten what Germany was like at the beginning of the nineteenth century, disjointed, vague and sentimental, for all the sporadic flames of its music and philosophy? And have we forgotten how Germany in a generation reached the wonderful maturity that preceded that plunge into imperialism which the bad old ways of the nineteenth century alone rendered inevitable? Our localists, our individualists, our American decentralizers may, if they choose, regard that process as an evil one, but if so they deny Goethe, the poet who, coöperating as it were with the Napoleonic wars, brought its dynamic unity to the German people. How did he do this? By projecting, in *Faust*, a personification of spiritual energy anchored by a long chain of specific incidents in the concrete experience of the German people and thereby infusing into that experience the leaven of development, impelling the individual to form himself into a peculiar being ever in search also of a conception of what men are collectively. By thus laying more and ever more demands upon human nature, by compelling men to accept that spirit of restless striving which gives them a leverage over things, he not only electrified the German people but obliged it to create an environment worthy of itself.

Now, it is of no importance at the moment that we have no Goethe in America and that we have no reason to suppose we are going to get one; it is of no importance that we cannot count on a messianic solution of our troubles. What is important is for us to see that the really effective approach to life is the poetic approach, the approach that Goethe summed up in his phrase "from within outward," and that it is the effective approach because it envisages method in terms of value, every ounce of pressure that is put upon value registering itself—to use the language of physics—with a tenfold intensity, so to speak, in the sphere of application.

This has been the European approach from time immemorial. Since the days of the cathedral-builders, everything that we call the environment has come as a natural result of the demands that human nature has laid upon itself. Is this less true of the present day than of the past? Has not the whole impetus toward social reform in modern England come about through that intensification of the poetic view of life which began with Carlyle's tremendous restatement of the spiritual principle, which passed over into the economic sphere with Ruskin and William Morris, and through which English liberalism has since learned gradually but effectively to assimilate science and use it as a ship uses a search-light? Can any of our awakeners take exception to the following passage in which Morris, actuated by his own lusty, creative joy in life and by his hatred, his vivid, compelling hatred of the ugliness of modern society, pointed out the path to reform from within outward?—

It was my good luck only that has put me on this side of the window among delightful books and lovely works of art, and not on the other side, in the empty street, the drink-steeped liquor shops, the foul and degraded lodgings. *I know by my own feelings and desires* what these men want, what could have saved them from this lowest depth of savagery: employment which would foster their self-respect, and win the prasie and sympathy of their fellows, and dwellings which they would come to with pleasure, surroundings which would soothe and elevate them, reasonable labour, reasonable. rest. There is only one thing that can give them this—Art.

Thus Morris, with his conception of "joy in labour," threw out in the midst of a machine age a palpitant standard of living that may well, in the end, serve to delimit the function of the machine in English society. And he did this, precisely, by the "unrealistic" method of projecting a Utopia, by seeing life in terms of that imagination which knows how important the intelligence is and is able to impel it in the direction of a deeply desired goal. That Morris knew little of science, and cared little for it, is beside the point; by laying demands upon life, by insisting that human nature must be creative, he obliged his contemporaries and his successors to frame *through* science an environment that would make that consummation possible. That is why the English liberalism represented in various ways by Shaw and Wells and Graham Wallas is so much more effective than the liberalism of our awakeners, who, while they have assimilated the ideas of all these men, have been unable to share their impulse. Shaw and Wells and Wallas, all of whom are as much the heirs of Morris's peculiar socialism as they are of science, have ever envisaged evolution in terms of a more stringent demand upon life; not in terms of fine thinking merely but of "love and fine thinking," not in terms of man merely but of self-surpassing man, not in terms of efficiency merely but of happiness, and all the other things have been added unto them—the things which have made possible, for instance, that beautiful programme of the British Labour Party over which we were all marvelling the other day.* Is it not a sufficient comment on our pragmatic awakeners that, possessing no infectious ideal of "joy in labour," the best they can do is to publish unleavened studies on the control of fatigue?

* 1917.

III

"I know by my own feelings and desires." Why has no one been able to embrace our American life in those dynamic personal terms with which Morris embraced the life of England? Why has it been impossible for us to compass the poetic view of life that has proved itself in other countries capable of so many wonderful things? It is because we have never been able to make any complicated imaginative demand upon life. Our field of reality has required such as over-development of our acquisitive instincts that our creative instincts have had no scope at all; and consequently we have never been able to rise above those two equally uncreative conceptions of human nature, the "total depravity" of Puritanism and that optimistic self-complacency which is Puritanism's obverse and twin brother. Instead of a Carlyle we have had an Emerson, instead of a Morris we have had a Whitman —that is the whole story.

For Emerson's private perfectibility, based as it was on the idea that all we have to do to attain our majority is to look within ourselves and cast off the swaddling-clothes of tradition, led by an easy transition, our society being what it was in the nineteenth century, into that conception of the "spontaneous man" which our political democracy had inherited from Rousseau and which, splendidly amplified by Walt Whitman, has weathered all the vicissitudes of our thinking to the present day. Not that one means to disparage Emerson, whose lofty and permanent place in the world of the spirit can only become more marked as time goes on. Not that one means to disparage Walt Whitman, who has taught us all to accept life and rejoice in it: one has only to recall that up to a generation ago our race was conceived in the holy shame of a reluctant wedlock to realize the extent of our national obligation to Whitman's robust animal humours. But greater as Whitman was than William Morris, he fulfilled a more primitive need, a need that would never have existed had it not been for our exclusively Puritan past; he was unable to carry us a step forward as Morris carried England, because, having embraced life, he was unable really to make anything of it. Where Morris, with his conception of "joy in labour," not only released the creative energies of men but held out before them a vision of excellence in labour that mobilized those energies and impelled men to reconstruct their environment in order to give them full play, Whitman merely universalized the miraculous animality that summed up his own experience. He knew nothing of what has been made of life, he was unable to imagine what can be made of life, over and above this miraculous animality. "Glad to be alive" simply, however intensely, he established a point of departure for the creative spirit—and there he left us. And there, so far as our poetical tradition is concerned, we have remained.

I resume all this because it explains why the pragmatists inherit no dynamic faith and why, lacking a dynamic faith, their treatment of society is itself so ineffective. It is in this lack of dynamic faith that they betray their unbroken descent from our old reformers and prove that pragmatism has not been the vital departure in our life that we have all been looking for. For what does it matter that our old reformers, ignorant of science, took for granted a "normal" human nature that was domestic and acquisitive, while our awakeners of the present day, equipped with a consummate scientific knowledge of mankind, take for granted a normal human nature that is efficient and sophisticated? At bottom they are all chips of the same block. Whittier, having risen to the heights of passion over the question of slavery, relapsed as soon as the war was over into a normal scale of values that enabled him, with whatever genial charm, to record, in *Snow-Bound*, his glowing satisfaction with things as they are, or were. The muckrakers of a later day having, at the rate of ten cents a word, abolished Peruna out of the world, passed on purified into the happy sphere in which Ray Stannard Baker wrote his *Adventures in Contentment*. And so it has been with the social workers, useful as they are, pragmatists one and all. Impelled to "give the other fellow a chance" to rise to the tepid status which life has portioned out to them, and which they regard as highly fortunate, they have carried things to such a pass that immigrant sociologists, under the stimulus of a middle-class journalism, have been known to regard it as the highest dream of their hearts to be able to "lift" to the level of some ordinary American suburban circle, into which they themselves have gained admittance, men and women who are often immeasurably above it in the scale of the spirit.

This question of our immigrant population affords, I think, the most critical test of any merely pragmatic sociology. Our "hyphenates," bred in a richly poetic, a richly creative soil, desire to live poetically and creatively; but they come to us as the detached limbs of a tree that they have left behind them. Has it never occurred to our pragmatists that the only way in which we can absorb their life is by providing them with a new tree upon which they can engraft themselves, and that the only hope of accomplishing this lies, not in improving their environment, in offering them comfort, in minimizing fatigue and shortening hours of work—important as all these things are, by the way—but in quickening our own consciousness, in puncturing our own complacency, in rising by the force of our own demands upon life to that sphere of joyous activity where we ourselves are able to shed light and communicate warmth? This a pragmatic sociology cannot accomplish; nor can it be accomplished except through an appeal from sociology to the higher court of literature. Incapable of the poetic view of life and repudiating it, the pragmatists are able to codify our society, to rearrange the allegiances that already exist, and to impose upon the American people programmes which have sprung from the poetic vision of other countries and which they have assimilated through their intelligence alone. Self-sufficient as they are, committed by the weakness of their imagination and by the analytic habit of their minds to a mechanistic view of human nature, they are unable to fuse and unify our wills, they are unable to communicate any of those vital incentives which are the austere fruits not of "interest" but of love. Did I say that, possessing no infectious ideal of "joy in labour," the best they can do is to concentrate their minds on the control of fatigue? No, they can do one thing better; they can evade reality altogether and say with Henry Ford that "no man can take pride in his work *until* he gets something for it, *until* he has leisure to enjoy life." In this way, throwing up the sponge altogether, accepting machinery and more machinery and still more machinery as a *fait accompli*, and giving up all hope of determining the rational place of machinery in life, they can tell their countrymen to seek reality in anything else than their work—in driving about the country in Ford cars, on Sundays, for example, with their mouths open.

Such is the destiny of the working class, as our young pragmatic intellectuals see it. As to the middle class, they can in time, by consummating their freedom and capping it with control, attain the more discreet paradise that the Pierce-Arrow Company is at last able to place at their disposal.

IV

So, becalmed as we are on a rolling sea, flapping and fluttering, hesitating and veering about, oppressed with a faint nausea, is it strange that we have turned mutinous not only against our old leaders, the minor prophets of Wall Street and their literary and philosophical standard-bearers, but also against our awakeners, the pragmatists, and the human nature that they wish to liberate in its own vicious circle, a human nature impoverished by hard, primitive conditions which has fulfilled the prophecy John Stuart Mill made with regard to industrialism in general, that it threatened the world with a "deficiency of preferences"?

Let us put it to our awakeners themselves. They say that we are born too late in a world too old to be able to compass anew the poetic view of life that has actuated the societies of Europe. They say that our blood is too mixed and our aims too diverse for us to achieve a national faith in the European sense. But what are they able to suggest as a substitute? We have no American culture, no; but we have an "American spirit," the spirit which has produced Sousa's music and Howard Chandler Christy's art and Mrs. Eddy's religion. Are they satisfied with this? We have none of the unity that gives life, no; but we have almost succumbed to the uniformity that destroys it. Are they pleased with this? Whether they subscribe to the "melting-pot" theory or believe in "preaching hyphenation," have they not proved themselves, in fact, bankrupt in solutions? They have, and it is because they have not entered into themselves, these awakeners of ours. "I know by my own feelings and desires," said Morris of the English workingmen of his time, "what these men want." When we have "feelings and desires," when, rather, we have poets to formulate them, to create for us emblems of a greater life, magnetic ideals grounded in our own field of reality, then our social problems, effectively handled by the very minds that fumble now because they cannot distinguish between ideals and methods, will begin to solve themselves.

Let no one imagine then that we have outgrown the poetic view of life; we have simply not grown up to it, we have not yet reached that full consciousness where faith and purpose, the hallmarks of the mature kind, are able to subjugate to their own ends the machinery of existence. "For life to be fruitful," said George Sand, "life must be felt as a blessing." But to love life, to perceive the miraculous beauty of life, and to seek for life, swiftly and effectively, a setting worthy of its beauty—this is the acme of civilization, to be attained, whether by individuals or by nations, only through a long and arduous process. But is it not true that human nature, at bottom the same the world over and at all times, irresistibly desires life and growth? And is it not true that human nature, in its infinite complexity, responds now with one set of faculties, now with another, according to circumstances and the quality of its leadership? If our poetic life is at present in the most rudimentary state and beset with fallacies of every kind, consider what our circumstances have been, and remember that our leadership in the past has not only not encouraged our poetic life, but has over-stimulated those very elements in our character that most retard its development.

VI. TOWARDS THE FUTURE

So I return to the beginning of my enquiry. An organized higher life: that is what the world demands of us, that is what we have at last come to demand of ourselves.

An organized higher life—in other words, in the first place, a literature fully aware of the difficulties of the American situation and able, in some sense, to meet them. For poets and novelists and critics are the pathfinders of society; to them belongs the vision without which the people perish. Our literature in the past has failed to produce sufficient minds capable of taking that supreme initiative; in consequence, it has fallen by its own weight under the chaos of our life. But for this it has not only the best of excuses, it has also at least one extraordinary precedent. Could there be a stranger parallel to the state of our literature today than the state of German literature in 1795, as Goethe describes it in the following words?—

> Germany is absolutely devoid of any central point of social culture, where authors might associate with one another and develop themselves by following, each in his own special branch, one aim, one common purpose. Born in places far remote from one another, educated in all

manner of ways, dependent as a rule upon themselves alone and upon the impressions of widely different surroundings; carried away by a predilection in favour of this or that example of native or foreign literature, driven to all kinds of attempts, nay, even blunders in their endeavour to test their own powers without proper guidance; brought to the conviction, gradually and only after much reflection, that they ought to adopt a certain course, and taught by practice what they can actually do; ever and anon confused and led astray by a large public devoid of taste and ready to swallow the bad with the same relish with which it has previously swallowed the good—is there any German writer of note who does not recognize himself in this picture, and who will not acknowledge with modest regret the many times that he has sighed for the opportunity of subordinating at an earlier stage of his career the peculiarities of his original genius to a general national culture, which, alas! was nowhere to be found? For the development of the higher classes by other moral influences and foreign literature, despite the great advantage which we have derived therefrom, has nevertheless hindered the Germans, as Germans, from developing themselves at an earlier stage.

How keenly our conscientious writers of the older generation must have experienced that regret, those, I mean, who have never quite submitted to the complacent colonialism that has marked so much of our culture in the past! But, unfortunately, they have left few testimonies behind them. They have considered it so much an obligation to justify American life merely as American life that they have glossed over their own tragedies, not realizing perhaps that in this way they have glossed over also the failure of those higher aims that they themselves were born to represent. "Not the fruit of experience, but experience itself, is the end." That is the essential European doctrine, and it is because Europeans value life as such that so great a part of their vital energy goes into the production of minds capable of heightening that value, minds that are able to keep the ball of life rolling in the sight and to the glory of all. But that, as I have tried to show, was not the doctrine of our forbears; quite the contrary, indeed. In consequence, the writers of the younger generation inherit all the difficulties of their elders, and at compound interest.

For the intellectual life is sustained by the emotional life; in order to react vigorously against one's environment one must in some degree have been emotionally nurtured by it. Our gifted minds lack too generally a certain sort of character without which talent is altogether fickle and fugitive; but what is this character if it is not the accumulated assurance, the spiritual force that results from preceding generations of effort along the lines towards which talent directs us? Professor Brückner points out in his history of Russian literature that "the direct transition from uncultured strata to strenuous mental activity is wont to avenge itself: the individual succumbs sooner or later to the unwonted burden." And as for so many of our young people, how often do they not wear themselves out constructing the preliminary platform without which it is impossible to create anything! We have so few ideals given us that the facts of our life do not instantly belie. Is it strange, therefore, that we have, unlike the peoples of Europe, no student class united in a common discipline and forming a sort of natural breeding-ground for the leadership that we desire?

Nevertheless, a class like this we must have, and there are, I think, many signs that such a class is rapidly coming into existence. To begin with, the sudden contraction of the national cultures of Europe during the war, owing to which many currents of thought, formerly shared by all, have been withdrawn as it were from circulation, has thrown us unexpectedly back upon ourselves. How many drafts we have issued in the past upon European thought, unbalanced by any investment of our own! The younger generation have come to feel this obligation acutely. At the same time they have been taught to speak a certain language in common by the social movements of the last twenty years. Acquainted through study and travel with ranges of human possibility which their ancestors were able to contemplate only in the abstract, they feel that the time has come to explore these possibilities and to test them out on our own soil. They see that Americans have seldom dreamed of a radically more beautiful civilization, our Utopias having been so generally of the nature of Edward Bellamy's, complex and ingenious mechanisms, liberating the soul into a vacuum of ennui. They see that it is art and literature which give the soul its higher values and make life worthy of intercession, and that every effective social revolution has been led up to and inspired by visionary leaders who have shown men what they might become and what they miss in living as they do. "Thought," according to one of the greatest of modern philosophers, "is strong enough to disturb the sense of satisfaction with nature; it is too weak to construct a new world in opposition to it." Only desire can do this, they feel, these Americans of the new age; that is what separates them not only from our traditional leaders, but also from our awakeners, the pragmatists, who are so busily unfolding the social order of which they form an integral part.

They feel this, I say; they feel it very deeply. How deeply they desire another America, not like the America of today, *grande et riche, mais désordonnée*, as Turgenev said of Russia, but harmonious and beneficent, a great America that knows how to use the finest of its gifts! And have they not seen, rising about them on the wings of a warm, humane, concerted endeavour, nation after nation, casting off whatever incubus of crabbed age, paralysis, tyranny, stupidity and sloth has lain most heavily upon the people's life, checking the free development of personality, retarding the circulation of generous ideas? The Young Italy of Mazzini's day, the Young Ireland of ours, the rebirth of the submerged nationalities of Eastern Europe, reborn not to the greater glory of imperialism but in the name of an incalculably rich international humanity that beckons from the future—have they witnessed again and again that sudden fusion of great natural aggregations of men by which all their elements have been set beating together at the highest pitch, without feeling, to the bottom of their hearts, that civilization ought to be a symphony and that there is in mankind an orchestral instinct that is even now clamouring at the gates of consciousness?

I do not say that there is in this anything that promises unison for us. Too many of the best minds of our own younger generation have already, owing to the aridity of our cultural soil, fallen victims to the creeping paralysis of the mechanistic view of life. Too many, more poetically endowed, have lost themselves in a confused and feeble anarchism. Too few Americans are able even to imagine what it means to be employed by civilization.

But certainly no true social revolution will ever be possible in America till a race of artists, profound and sincere, has brought us face to face with our own experience and set working in that experience the leaven of the highest culture. For it is exalted desires that give their validity to revolutions, and exalted desires take form only in exalted souls. But has there ever been a time when masses of men have conceived these desires without leaders appearing to formulate them and press them home? We are lax now, too lax, because we do not realize the responsibility that lies upon us, each in the measure of his own gift. Is it imaginable, however, that as time goes on and side by side with other nations we come to see the inadequacy of our own, we shall fail to rise to the gravity of our situation and recreate, out of the sublime heritage of human ideals, a new synthesis adaptable to the unique conditions of our life?

When that occurs, we shall begin to grow, as a people; and having begun to grow we shall grow quickly. For we already possess elements that belong to every level of development, even the highest; we possess them all, but they are not grouped in a vital order, they have no cumulative significance. As soon as the foundations of our life have been reconstructed and made solid on the basis of an experience of which we have been shown the potentialities, all these extraneous, ill-regulated forces will rally about their newly-found centre; they will fit in, each where it belongs, contributing to the architecture of our life. Then, and only then, shall we cease to be a blind, selfish, disorderly people. We shall become a luminous people, dwelling in the light and sharing our light.

their validity in [illegible], and exalted desires take form only in exalted souls. But has there ever been a time when masses of men have conceived these desires without leaders appearing to formulate them and press them home? We are unhappy, but lax, because we do not realise the responsibility that lies upon us each in the measure of his own gift. Is it conceivable that as time goes on [illegible] side by side with other nations we come to see the mad race of our own, we shall fail to rise to the gravity of our situation and remake, put into the sublime heritage of human ideals a new significance adaptable to the unique condition of our life?

When that is done we shall begin to grow as a people and when we begin to grow we shall grow quickly. The world already possesses elements that belong to every stage of development, even the highest. We possess them all but they are not grouped in a vital organ: they have no cumulative significance. As soon as the tendencies of our life have been recognized and made solid in the ideas of an experience in which we have been shown the potentialities, all these diverse and ill-organized forces will rally about their newly found centre; they will fit in each where it belongs, contributing to the circumference of our life. Then, and only then, shall we cease to be a blind, selfish, disorderly people. We shall become a unanimous people, dwelling in thought and standing out right.

The Literary Life in America

1921

THE LITERARY LIFE IN AMERICA

AMONG all the figures which, in Edith Wharton's *The Age of Innocence*, make up the pallid little social foreground, the still more pallid middle distance, of the New York of forty years ago, there is none more pallid than the figure of Ned Winsett, the "man of letters untimely born in a world that had no need of letters." Winsett, we are told, "had published one volume of brief and exquisite literary appreciations," of which one hundred and twenty copies had been sold, and had then abandoned his calling and taken an obscure post on a woman's weekly. "On the subject of *Hearth-fires* (as the paper was called) he was inexhaustibly entertaining," says Mrs. Wharton; "but beneath his fun lurked the sterile bitterness of the still young man who has tried and given up." Sterile bitterness, a bright futility, a beginning without a future: that is the story of Ned Winsett.

One feels, as one turns Mrs. Wharton's pages, how symbolic this is of the literary life in America. I shall say nothing of the other arts, though the vital conditions of all the arts have surely much in common; I shall say nothing of America before the Civil War, for the America that New England dominated was a different nation from ours. But what immediately strikes one, as one surveys the history of our literature during the last half century, is the singular impotence of its creative spirit. That we have and have always had an abundance of talent is, I think, no less evident: what I mean is that so little of this talent really finds its way. Of how many of our modern writers can it be said that their work reveals a continuous growth, or indeed any growth, that they hold their ground tenaciously and preserve their sap from one decade to another? Where, to speak relatively, the characteristic evolution of the European writer is one of an ever-increasing differentiation, a progress towards the creation, the possession of a world absolutely his own (the world of Shaw, the world of Hardy, the world of Hamsun, of Gorky, of Anatole France), the American writer, having struck out with his new note, becomes—how often! —progressively less and less himself. The blighted career, the arrested career, the diverted career are, with us, the rule. The chronic state of our literature is that of a youthful promise which is never redeemed.

The great writer, the *grand écrivain*, has at the best of times appeared but once or twice in America: that is another matter. I am speaking, as I say, of the last half century, and I am speaking of the rank and file. There are those who will deny this characterization of our literature, pointing to what they consider the robust and wholesome corpus of our "normal" fiction. But this fiction, in its way, corroborates my point. What is the quality of the spirit behind it? How much does it contain of that creative element the character of which consists in dominating life instead of being dominated by it? Have these novelists of ours any world of their own as distinguished from the world they observe and reflect, the world they share with their neighbours? Is it a personal vision that informs them, or a mob-vision? The Danish writer, Johannes V. Jensen, has described their work as "journalism under exceptionally fortunate conditions." Journalism, on the whole, it assuredly is, and the chief of these fortunate conditions (fortunate for journalism!) has been the general failure of the writers in question to establish and develop themselves as individuals: as they have rendered unto Cæsar what was intended for God, is it any wonder that Cæsar has waxed so fat? "The unfortunate thing," writes Montrose J. Moses, "is that the American drama"—and the observation is equally true of this fiction of ours—"has had many brilliant promises which have finally thinned out and never materialized." And again: "The American dramatist has always taken his logic at second hand; he has always allowed his theatrical sense to be a slave to managerial circumstance." The two statements are complementary, and they apply, as I say, to the whole of this "normal" literature. Managerial circumstance? Let us call it local patriotism, the spirit of the times, the hunger of the public for this, that or the other: to some one of these demands, these promptings from without, the "normal" American writer always allows himself to become a slave. It is the fact, indeed, of his being a slave to some demand from without that makes him "normal"—and something else than an artist.

The flourishing exterior of the main body of our contemporary literature, in short, represents anything but the integrity of an inner well-being. But even aside from this, one can count on one's two hands the American writers who are able to carry on the development and unfolding of their individualities, year in, year out, as every competent man of affairs carries on his business. What fate overtakes the rest? Shall I begin to run over some of those names, familiar to us all, names that have signified so much promise and are lost in what Gautier calls "the limbo where moan (in the company of babes) still-born vocations, abortive attempts, larvæ of ideas that have won neither wings nor shapes"? Shall I mention the writers—but they are countless!—who have lapsed into silence or involved themselves in barren eccentricities, or who have been turned into machines? The poets who, at the outset of their careers, find themselves extinguished like so many candles? The novelists who have been unable to grow up, and remain withered boys of seventeen? The critics who find themselves overtaken in mid-career by a hardening of the spiritual arteries? Our writers all but universally lack the power of growth, the endurance that enables one to continue to produce personal work after the freshness of youth has gone.

Such is the aspect of our contemporary literature; beside that of almost any European country, it is indeed one long list of spiritual casualties. For it is not that the talent is wanting, but that somehow this talent fails to fulfil itself.

This being so, how much one would like to assume, with certain of our critics, that the American writer is a sort of Samson bound with the brass fetters of the Philistines and requiring only to have those fetters cast off in order to be able to conquer the world! That, as I understand it, is the position of Theodore Dreiser, who recently remarked of certain of our novelists: "They succeeded in writing but one book before the iron hand of convention took hold of them." There is this to be said for the argument, that if the American writer as a type shows less resistance than the European writer it is plainly because he has been insufficiently equipped, stimulated, nourished by the society into which he has been born. In this sense, the American environment is answerable for the literature it has produced. But what is significant is that the American writer *does* show less resistance; and as literature is nothing but the expression of power, of the creative will, of "free will," in short, is it not more accurate to say, not that the "iron hand of convention" takes hold of our writers, but that our writers yield to the "iron hand of convention"? Samson had lost his virility before the Philistines bound him; it was because he had lost his virility that the Philistines were able to bind him. The American writer who "goes wrong" is in a similar case. "I have read," says Dreiser, of Jack London, "several short stories which proved what he could do. But he did not feel that he cared for want and public indifference. Hence his many excellent romances." *He did not feel that he cared for want and public indifference.* Even Dreiser, as we observe, determinist that he is, admits a margin of free will, for he represents Jack London as having made a choice. What concerns us now, however, is not a theoretical but a practical question, the fact, namely, that the American writer as a rule is actuated not by faith but by fear, that he cannot meet the obstacles of "want and public indifference" as the European writer meets them, that he is, indeed, and as if by nature, a journeyman and a hireling.

As we see, then, the creative will in this country is a weak and sickly plant. Of the innumerable talents that are always emerging about us there are few that come to any sort of fruition. The rest wither early; they are transformed into those neuroses that flourish on our soil as orchids flourish in the green jungle. The sense of this failure is written all over our literature. Do we not know what depths of disappointment underlay the cynicism of Mark Twain and Henry Adams and Ambrose Bierce? Have we failed to recognize, in the surly contempt with which the author of *The Story of a Country Town* habitually speaks of writers and writing, the unconscious cry of sour grapes of a man whose creative life was arrested in youth? Are we unaware of the bitterness with which, in certain letters of his later years, Jack London regretted the miscarriage of his gift? There is no denying that for half a century the American writer as a type has gone down to defeat.

Now, why is this so? Why does the American writer, relatively speaking, show less resistance than the European writer? Plainly, as I have just said, because he has been insufficiently equipped, stimulated, nourished by the society into which he has been born. If our creative spirits are unable to grow and mature, it is a sign that there is something wanting in the soil from which they spring and the conditions that surround them. Is it not, for that matter, a sign of some more general failure in our life?

"At the present moment," wrote G. K. Chesterton in one of his early essays (*The Fallacy of the Young Nation*), struck by the strange anæmia of so many American artists, "at the present moment the matter which America has very seriously to consider is not how near it is to its birth and beginning, but how near it may be to its end. . . . The English colonies have produced no great artists, and that fact may prove that they are still full of silent possibilities and reserve force. But America has produced great artists and that fact most certainly means that she is full of a fine futility and the end of all things. Whatever the American men of genius are, they are not young gods making a young world. Is the art of Whistler a brave, barbaric art, happy and headlong? Does Mr. Henry James infect us with the spirit of a school-boy? No, the colonies have not spoken, and they are safe. Their silence may be the silence of the unborn. But out of America has come a sweet and startling cry, as unmistakable as the cry of a dying man." That there is some truth behind this, that the soil of our society is arid and impoverished, is indicated by the testimony of our own poets. One has only to consider what George Cabot Lodge wrote in 1904 in one of his letters: "We are a dying race, as every race must be of which the men are, as men and not accumulators, third-rate"; one has only to consider the writings of Messrs. Frost, Robinson and Masters, in whose presentation of our life, in the West as well as in the East, the individual as a spiritual unit invariably suffers defeat. Fifty years ago, J. A. Froude, on a visit to this country, wrote to one of his friends: "From what I see of the Eastern states I do not anticipate any very great things as likely to come out of the Americans. . . . They are generous with their money, they have tenderness and quiet good humour; but the Anglo-Saxon power is running to seed and I don't think will revive." When we consider the colourlessness and insipidity of our latter-day life (faithfully reflected in the novels of Howells and his successors), the absence from it of profound passions and intense convictions, of any representative individuals who can be compared in spiritual force with Emerson, Thoreau and so many of their contemporaries, its uniformity and its uniform tepidity, then the remark of John Jay Chapman, "Our age has been an age of management, not of ideas or of men," assumes indeed a very sinister import. I go back to the poet Lodge's letters. "Was there ever," he writes, "such an anomaly as the American man? In practical affairs his cynicism, energy and capacity are simply stupefying, and in every other respect he is a sentimental idiot possessing neither the interest, the capacity nor the desire for even the most elementary processes of independent thought. . . . His wife finds him so sexually inapt that she refuses to bear him children and so drivelling in every way except as a money-getter that she compels him to expend his energies solely in that direction while she leads a discontented, sterile, stunted life." Is this to be denied? And does it not in part explain that lovelessness of the American scene which has bred the note of a universal resentment in so much of our contemporary fiction? As well expect figs from thistles as men from such a soil who are robust enough to prefer spiritual to material victories and who are capable of achieving them.

It is unnecessary to go back to Taine in order to realize that here we have a matrix as unpropitious as possible for literature and art. If our writers wither early, if they are too generally pliant, passive, acquiescent, anæmic, how much is this not due to the heritage of pioneering, with its burden of isolation, nervous strain, excessive work and all the racial habits that these have engendered?

Certainly, for example, if there is anything that counts in the formation of the creative spirit it is that long infancy to which John Fiske, rightly or wrongly, attributed the emergence of man from the lower species. In the childhood of almost every great writer one finds this protracted incubation, this slow stretch of years in which the unresisting organism opens itself to the influences of life. It was so with Hawthorne, it was so with Whitman in the pastoral America of a century ago: they were able to mature, these brooding spirits, because they had given themselves for so long to life before they began to react upon it. That is the old-world childhood still, in a measure; how different it is from the modern American childhood may be seen if one compares, for example, the first book ("Boyhood") of *Pelle the Conqueror* with any of those innumerable tales in which our novelists show us that in order to succeed in life one cannot be up and doing too soon. The whole temper of our society, if one is to judge from these documents, is to hustle the American out of his childhood, teaching him at no age at all how to repel life and get the best of it and build up the defences behind which he is going to fight for his place in the sun. Who can deny that this racial habit succeeds in its unconscious aim—to produce sharp-witted men of business? But could anything be deadlier to the poet, the artist, the writer?

Everything in such an environment, it goes without saying, tends to repress the creative and to stimulate the competitive impulses. A certain Irish poet has observed that all he ever learned of poetry he got from talking with peasants along the road. Whitman might have said almost as much, even of New York, the New York of seventy years ago. But what nourishment today can the receptive spirit find in the harassed, inhibited mob of our fellow-countrymen, eaten up with the "itch of ill-advised activity"—what encouragement to become anything but automatons like themselves? And what direction, in such a society, does the instinct of emulation receive, that powerful instinct of adolescence? A certain visitor of Whitman's has described him as living in a house "as cheerless as an ash-barrel," a house indeed "like that in which a very destitute mechanic" might have lived. Is it not symbolic, that picture, of the esteem in which our democracy holds the poet? If today the man of many dollars is no longer the hero of the editorial page and the baccalaureate address, still, or rather more than ever, it is the "aggressive" type that overshadows every corner of our civilization; the intellectual man who has gone his own way was never less the hero. Many, in short, are the elements in our society that contribute to form a selection constantly working against the survival of the creative type.

It is certainly true that none of these unfavourable conditions could have had such a baleful effect upon our literature if there had been others to counteract them. An aristocratic tradition, if we had ever had it, would have kept open among us the right of way of the free individual, would have preserved the claims of mere living. "It is curious to observe," writes Nietzsche in one of his letters, "how anyone who soon leaves the traditional highway in order to travel on his own proper path always has more or less the sense of being an exile, a condemned criminal, a fugitive from mankind." If that is true in the old world, where society is so much more complex and offers the individual so much more latitude, how few could ever have had the strength, in a society like ours, which has always placed such a premium on conformity, to become and remain themselves? Is it fanciful indeed to see in the famous "remorse" of Poe the traces left by this dereliction of the tribal law on the unconscious mind of an artist of unique force and courage? Similarly, a tradition of voluntary poverty would have provided us with an escape from the importunities of bourgeois custom. But aside from the fact that even so simple a principle as this depends largely for its life on precedent (Whitman and the painter Ryder are almost alone among latter-day Americans in having discovered it for themselves), aside from the fact that to secede from the bourgeois system is, in America, to subject oneself to quite peculiar penalties (did it ever occur to Mark Twain that he *could* be honourably poor?)—aside from all this, poverty in the new world is not the same thing as poverty in the old: one has only to think of Charles Lamb and all the riches that London freely gave him, all the public resources he had at his disposal, to appreciate the difference. With us poverty means in the end an almost inevitable intellectual starvation. Consider such a plaint as Sidney Lanier's: "I could never describe to you" (he writes to Bayard Taylor) "what a mere drought and famine my life has been, as regards that multitude of matters which I fancy one absorbs when one is in an atmosphere of art, or when one is in conversational relationship with men of letters, with travellers, with persons who have either seen, or written, or done large things. Perhaps you know that, with us of the younger generation in the South since the war, pretty much the whole of life has been merely not dying." That is what poverty means in America, poverty and isolation, for Lanier, whose talent, as we can see today, was hopelessly crippled by it, was mistaken if he supposed that there was anything peculiar to the South in that plight of his: it has been the plight of the sensitive man everywhere in America and at all times. Add to poverty the want of a society devoted to intellectual things and we have such a fate as Herman Melville's in New York. "What he lacked," says Frank Jewett Mather, "was possibly only health and nerve, but perhaps, even more, companionship of a friendly, critical, understanding sort. In London, where he must have been hounded out of his corner, I can imagine Melville carrying the reflective vein to literary completion." Samuel Butler was not entirely mistaken when he jotted down the following observation in his notebook: "America will have her geniuses, as every other country has, in fact she has already had one in Walt Whitman, but I do not think America is a good place in which to be a genius. A genius can never expect to have a good time anywhere, if he is the genuine article, but America is about the last place in which life will be endurable at all for an inspired writer of any kind."

To such circumstances as these, I say, the weakness of our literary life is due. But the lack of great leaders, of a strong and self-respecting literary guild (the one results from the other)—is not this our chief misfortune? In the best of circumstances, and considering all the devils that beset the creative spirit, a strong impulse is scarcely enough to carry the writer through: he must feel not only that he is doing what he wishes to do, but that what he is doing *matters*. If dozens of American writers have fallen by the wayside because they have met with insuperable obstacles, dozens of others have fallen, with all their gifts, because they have lost interest in their work, because they have ceased to "see the necessity" of it. This is just the point where the presence of a leader, of a local tradition, a school, a guild, makes all the difference. "With the masters I converse," writes Gauguin in his journal. "Their example fortifies me. When I am tempted to falter I blush before them." If that could have been true of Gauguin, the "Wolf," who walked by himself as few have walked, what shall we say of other men whose artistic integrity, whose faith in themselves, is exposed every day to the corroding influences of a mechanized civilization? It would be all very well if literature were merely a mode of "having a good time": I am speaking of those, the real artists, who, with Nietzsche, make a distinction (illusory perhaps) between "happiness" and "work," and I say that these men have always fed on the thought of greatness and on the propinquity of greatness. It was not for nothing that Turgenev bore in his memory, as a talisman, the image of Pushkin; that Gorky, having seen Tolstoy once, sitting among the boulders on the seashore, felt everything in him blending in one happy thought, "I am not an orphan on the earth, so long as this man lives on it." The presence of such men immeasurably raises the morale of the literary life. That is what Chekhov meant when he said, "I am afraid of Tolstoy's death." And is it not true that the whole contemporary literature of England has drawn virtue from Thomas Hardy? The sense that one is *working in a great line*: this, more than anything else perhaps, renews one's confidence in the "quaint mania of passing one's life wearing oneself out over words," as Flaubert called it, in the still greater folly of pursuing one's ego when everything in life combines to punish one for doing so. The successful pursuit of the ego is what makes literature; this requires not only a certain inner intensity but also a certain courage, and it is doubtful whether, in any nation, any considerable number of men can summon up that courage and maintain it unless they have *seen the thing done*. The very notion that such a life is either possible or desirable, the notion that such a life exists even, can hardly occur to the rank and file: some individual has to start the ball rolling, some individual of extraordinary force and audacity, and where is that individual to be found in our modern American literature? Whitman is the unique instance, for Henry James was an exile; and Whitman was not only essentially of an earlier generation, he was an invalid who folded his hands in mid-career.

Of those others what can we say, those others whose gifts have fitted them to be our leaders? Howells once observed of the American drama that "mainly it has been gay as our prevalent mood is, mainly it has been honest, as our habit is, in cases where we believe we can afford it." In this gently ironical pleasantry one seems to discern the spirit of the literature of the age preceding ours. But it was Howells himself who, in order to arrive at the doctrine that "the more smiling aspects of life are the more American," deliberately, as he has told us, and professed realist that he was, averted his eyes from the darker side of life. And Mark Twain suppressed his real beliefs about man and the universe. And Henry Adams refused to sponsor in public the novels that revealed what he considered to be the truth about American society. At its very headwaters, as we see, this modern literature of ours has failed to flow clear: the creative impulse in these men, richly endowed as they were, was checked and compromised by too many other impulses, social and commercial. If one is to blame anything for this, it is the immense insecurity of our life, which is due to its chaotic nature; for one is not entitled to expect greatness even of those who have the greatest gifts, and of these men Adams was alone secure; of Howells and Mark Twain, frontiersmen as they were, it may be said that they were obliged to compromise, consciously or unconsciously, to gain a foothold in the one corner of the country where men were able to exist as writers at all. But if these men were unable to establish their independence (and one has only to recall the notorious Gorky dinner in order to perceive the ignominy of their position), what can one expect of the rank and file? Great men form a sort of windshield behind which the rest of their profession are able to build up their own defences; they establish a right of way for the others; they command a respect for their profession, they arouse in the public a concern for it, an interest in it, from which the others benefit. As things are, the literary guild in America is not greatly respected, nor does it too greatly respect itself. In *My Literary Passions,* Howells, after saying that his early reading gave him no standing among other boys, observes: "I have since found that literature gives one no more certain station in the world of men's activities, either idle or useful. We literary folk try to believe that it does, but that is all nonsense. At every period of life among boys or men we are accepted when they are at leisure and want to be amused, and at best we are tolerated rather than accepted." That is ironical too, but a little pathetic as well. Imagine Gorky or Hamsun or Bernard Shaw "trying to believe" that literature gives him a certain station in the world of men's activities! Howells, conscientious craftsman that he was, instinctively shared, in regard to the significance of his vocation, the feeling of our pragmatic philosophers, who justify the intellectual life by showing how useful it is. And then there is R. W. Chambers, who has remarked that writers "are not held in excessive esteem by really busy people, the general idea being—which is usually true—that literature is a godsend to those unfitted for real work." After this, one can easily understand why it is that our novelists take such pains to be mistaken for business men.

So much for the conditions, or at least a few of them, that have prevented our literature from getting its head above water. If America is littered with extinct talents, the halt, the maimed and the blind, it is for reasons with which we are all too familiar; and those to whom the creative life is the principle of human movement look on this wreckage of everything that is most precious to society and ask themselves what our fathers meant when they extolled the progress of our civilization. But let us look facts in the face. Sinclair Lewis says that we are in the midst of a revival and that we are too humble in supposing that our contemporary literature is inferior to that of England. That we are in the midst of a revival no one doubts, but it is the sustained career that makes a literature; without the evidence of this, we can hope much but we can affirm nothing. And what we can see is that, with all its hope, the morale of the literary profession in this country is just what its antecedents have made it. I am reminded of the observation of a friend who has reason to know, that the Catholic Church in America, great as it is in numbers and organization, still depends on the old world for its models, its taskmasters and its inspiration; for the American priest, as a rule, does not feel the vocation as the European feels it. I am reminded of the American workers' movement which, prosperous as it is in comparison with the workers' movements of Europe, is unparalleled for the feebleness of its representatives. I am reminded of certain brief experiences in the American university world which have led me to believe that the professors who radiate a genuine light and warmth are far more likely to be Russians, Germans, Englishmen, Dutchmen and Swedes than the children of 1776. The hostility of the pioneers to the special career still operates to prevent in the American mind the powerful, concentrated pursuit of any non-utilitarian way of life. Considered with reference to its higher manifestations, life itself has been thus far, in modern America, a failure. Of this the failure of our literature is merely emblematic.

H. L. Mencken, who shares this belief, urges that the only hope of a change for the better lies in the development of a native aristocracy that will stand between the writer and the public, supporting him, appreciating him, forming as it were a *cordon sanitaire* between the individual and the mob. That no change can come without the development of an aristocracy of some sort, some nucleus of the more gifted, energetic and determined, one can hardly doubt. But how can one expect the emergence of an aristocracy outside the creative class, and devoted to its welfare, unless and until the creative class itself reveals the sort of will that attracts its ministrations? "The notion that a people can run itself and its affairs anonymously is now well known to be the silliest of absurdities." Thus William James, in defence of the aristocratic principle; and what he says is as applicable to literature as to every other department of social life. But he continues: "Mankind does nothing save through initiatives on the part of inventors, great and small, and imitation by the rest of us—these are the sole factors alive in human progress. Individuals of genius show the way, and set the pattern, which common people then adopt and follow." In other words, so far as literature is concerned, the burden of proof lies on the writer himself—which brings one back to a truism: it is not for the public or any aristocratic minority within the public to understand the writer, it is for the writer to create the taste by which he is understood. Is it not by this indeed (in a measure, at least) that we recognize the creator?

Certainly if our contemporary literature is not respected, if it has not been able to rally to its support the sensitive public that exists in this country, it is partly because this literature has not respected itself. That there has been every reason for this makes no difference; that it has begun to respect itself again makes no difference either, for when a people has lost confidence in its literature, and has had grounds for losing confidence, one cannot be surprised if it insists upon being "shown." The public supported Mark Twain and Howells and the men of their generation, it admired them for what was admirable in them, but it was aware, if only unconsciously, that there was a difference between them and the men of the generation before them; and in consequence of this the whole stock of American literature fell. But those who insist in our day that America prefers European writers to its own, because America is still a colony of Europe, cannot ignore the significant fact that, at a time when America was still more truly colonial, American writers had all the prestige in this country that European writers have at present; and it is not entirely because at that time the country was more homogeneous. Poe and Thoreau found little support in the generation I speak of, as Whitman found little support in the generation that followed it. On the other hand, there were no European writers (and it was an age of great writers in Europe) who were held in higher esteem in this country than Hawthorne, Emerson, Motley and half a dozen others almost equally distinguished, as well from a European as from an American point of view; there were, in fact, few, if any, European writers who were esteemed in this country as highly as they. How can one explain it? How can one explain why, at a time when America, in every other department of life, was more distinctly colonial than it is now, American literature commanded the full respect of Americans, while today, when the colonial tradition is vanishing all about us, it so little commands their respect that they go after any strange god from England? The problem is far from simple, but among its many explanations one can hardly deny that there were in that period a number of writers of unusual power, who made the most of their power, and followed their artistic conscience, and who by this fact built up a public confidence in themselves and the literature they represented. Does it matter at all whether we today enjoy these writers or not? They were men of spiritual force: that is the important point. If the emerging writers of our epoch find themselves handicapped by the skepticism of the public, they have only to remember that they are themselves for the most part in the formative stage and that they have to live down the recent past of their profession.

Meanwhile, what constitutes a literature is the spiritual force of the individuals who compose it. If our literature is to grow, it can only be through the development of a sense of "free will" on the part of our writers themselves. To be, to feel oneself, a "victim" is in itself not to be an artist, for it is the nature of the artist to live, not in the world of which he is an effect, but in the world of which he is the cause, the world of his own creation. For this reason, the pessimistic determinism of the present age is, from the point of view of literature, of a piece with the optimistic determinism of the age that is passing. But this pessimistic determinism reveals a *consciousness of the situation:* to that extent it represents a gain, and one may even say that to be conscious of the situation is half the battle. If we owed nothing else to Theodore Dreiser, we should owe him enough for the tragic sense of the waste of American life which his books communicate. It remains true that, if we resent this life, it is only a sign of our weakness, of the harm we have permitted this civilization to do us, of our imperfectly realized freedom; for to the creative spirit in its free state the external world is merely an impersonal point of departure. Thus it is certain that as long as the American writers share what James Bryce called the "mass fatalism" of the American people, our literature will remain the sterile, inferior phenomenon which, on the whole, it is.

"What we want," wrote Henry Adams in 1862 to his brother Charles, "is a *school.* We want a national set of young men like ourselves or better, to start new influences not only in politics, but in literature, in law, in society, and throughout the whole social organism of the country—a national school of our own generation. And that is what America has no power to create. . . . It's all random, insulated work, for special and temporary and personal purposes. And we have no means, power or hope of combined action for any unselfish end." *That is what America has no power to create.* But can it be said that any nation has ever created a school? Here we have the perfect illustration of that mass fatalism of which I have spoken, and Henry Adams himself, in his passivity, is the type of it. Secure as he was, uniquely secure, why did he refuse to accept the responsibility of those novels in which he expressed the contempt of a powerful and cultivated mind for the meanness of the guiding element in American society? In the darkest and most chaotic hours of our spiritual history the individual has possessed a measure of free will only to renounce it: if Henry Adams had merely signed his work, he might by that very fact have become the founder of the school that he desired. But it is true that in that generation the impulses of youth were, with extraordinary unanimity, focussed upon a single end, the exploitation of the continent; the material opportunities that American life offered were too great and too all-engrossing, and it is unlikely that any considerable minority could have been rallied for any non-utilitarian cause. Sixty years later, this school remains the one thing necessary: the reforestation of our spiritual territory depends upon it. And in more than one sense the times are favourable. The closing of the frontier seems to promise for this country an intenser life than it has known before; a large element of the younger generation, estranged from the present order, exists in a state of ferment that renders it highly susceptible to new ideas; the country swarms with half-artists who have ceased to conform to the law of the tribe but have not accepted the discipline of their own individual spirits. "What I chiefly desire for you," wrote Ibsen to Brandes at the outset of his career, "is a genuine, full-blooded egoism, which shall force you for a time to regard what concerns you yourself as the only thing of any consequence, and everything else as non-existent. . . . There is no way in which you can benefit society more than by coining the metal you have in yourself." The second half of this rather blunt counsel of perfection is implied in the first, and it connotes a world of things merely to name which would be to throw into relief the infantility of the American writer as a type. By what prodigies of alert self-adaptation, of discrimination, self-scrutiny, conscious effort, does the creative will come into its own! As for ourselves, weak as too many of us are, ignorant, isolated, all too easily satisfied, and scarcely as yet immune from the solicitations of the mob, we still have this advantage, that an age of reaction is an age that stirs the few into a consciousness of themselves.

our spiritual literary [illegible] in general. And it must [illegible] of the [illegible] seems to [illegible] for this country [illegible] than it has hitherto [illegible] of the [illegible] [illegible] individual spirit. What is clearly dawning [illegible] which shall force [illegible] [illegible] As for ourselves [illegible] [illegible] consciousness of themselves.